Praise for TURNING INTERNATIONAL

"Being an international or an expat is not a science - but science can go a long way in understanding how to succeed at, enjoy and benefit from international living. Catherine takes her own personal experience, those of countless internationals as well as her profession (psychology) to explore the many dimensions of international living. The result: a book full of understanding and countless exercises designed to get internationals on the road to becoming happy and healthy."

> - Deborah Valentine, lifelong international, executive director Access Netherlands, www.ahandinthehague.com

"A must read for anyone who has moved abroad for the first time, whether as an Expat or on a permanent basis and is finding it harder than they anticipated. The varying real life examples help illustrate what may, once read, seem obvious but which, in the chaos and excitement of a move, may be completely overlooked.

Written by a psychologist it really provides an insight into the mental challenges people face without their family and friends around for support and the feelings that they may be going through. It provides in-depth knowledge as to how the feelings come about so they can be better understood and managed."

> - Brian Friedman, Founder and CEO The Forum for Expatriate Management, www.totallyexpat.com

"In her book Turning International Catherine Transler does a great job of addressing many of the challenges faced by those looking to build a new life in another country. She provides insight into what happens in the mind and body of a person experiencing stress and negative emotions to place her readers in a better position to constructively deal with them. In addition to useful exercises and models to understand how to best integrate into a new culture, she also explores the importance of social networks and how to build them to support a fulfilling life overseas.

I highly recommend this book to anyone interested in equipping themselves with knowledge and actionable guidance to overcome obstacles, deal with ongoing change and build resilience to not only survive but thrive in their life abroad."

- **Megan Fitzgerald, Expat and International Career Coach, www.careerbychoice.com**

"Turning International contributes to the conversation of living cross-culturally with an in-depth look at the psychological underpinnings of emotions and behaviors associated with the expatriate experience. Augmenting her own story with interviews of others, Catherine Transler explains the 'chemistry of loneliness', the physiological basis for feeling anxious when in a culture other than our own, and the need to reach out and widen our support networks for our physical and emotional well-being.

The chapter on Cultural Differences in Values and Attitudes across societies is particularly illuminating, showing why Turning International belongs on your bookshelf."

- **Linda A. Janssen, expat and co-author of Turning Points: 25 Inspiring Stories from Women Entrepreneurs, www.adventuresinexpatland.com**

" Transler has produced an essential guide to the realities we face when moving abroad, whether permanently or temporarily. Dealing clearly with the psychology of relocation, readers are taken step by step through the issues they may face. With a wealth of individual experience woven through the informative text, this book should be on the reading list of everyone planning their move to a new country."

- **Emmy Coffey Mccarthy,**
Best Expat of the Year 2012 in the Netherlands,
Founder and Director of Amsterdam Mamas.

TURNING INTERNATIONAL

TURNING INTERNATIONAL

How to Find Happiness and Feel at Home in a New Culture.

Catherine Transler, Ph.D.

Rotterdam, The Netherlands.

Turning International.

Copyright © 2012 Catherine Transler. All rights reserved. No part of this publication may be reproduced or distributed in any form or by any means, or stored in a database or retrieval system, without the prior written permission of the author.

Copyrights © Tables 6.2, 6.3, 6.4, 6.5, and 6.6: Geert Hofstede, Gert Jan Hofstede, Michael Minkov, "Cultures and Organizations, Software of the Mind," Third Revised Edition, McGrawHill 2010, ISBN 0-07-166418-1.Copyright Geert Hofstede B.V. Quoted with permission.

Copyrights © Picture page 122 Copyrights Shutterstock.com.

Cover design by Richard Fender, www.scenicroutesdesign.com.

De Zandloper Publications, Rotterdam, The Netherlands.

ISBN 978-90-818868-0-2.

De Koninklijke Bibliotheek, Den Haag, NL.

- Psychologie algemeen (770).

Print on Demand.

Half of the profits from this book sales will go to KIVA, an international organization that provides loans to working men and women who live in poverty.
www.Kiva.org

Contents

Warning and Disclaimer 4

PART 1. INNER JOURNEY

Chapter 1. My Story 8
Chapter 2. The Arrival 16
Chapter 3. Loneliness 42
Chapter 4. Acculturation Stress and Chronic Stress 55
Chapter 5. Home Abroad 75

PART 2. SOCIAL LIFE

Chapter 6. Cultural Differences in Values and Attitudes 90
Chapter 7. New Language and New Interactions 124
Chapter 8. From Strangers to Friends 145
Chapter 9. Integration and Support Networks 162

PART 3. BALANCED LIFE

Chapter 10. Finding Strength, Meaning, and Balance 188
Chapter 11. Enjoying Life Abroad 201
Epilogue 206

REFERENCES 211
RESOURCES 218
APPENDIX 221
ACKNOWLEDGMENTS 231
ABOUT THE AUTHOR 233

Warning and Disclaimer

The book is designed to provide guidelines for improving the quality of life and well-being of everybody who has lived or intends to live abroad. It is based on positive-psychology methods, which are intended to ameliorate the quality of life and performance of people who do not have particular mental health or physical health issues. It is not intended as a substitute for diagnosis or for advice from a psychologist, medical doctor, psychiatrist, or trained therapist. If you experience feelings of depression or suffer from addictions, fatigue, physical pains, or any type of mental or physical symptoms, you should seek professional assistance.

"Internationals" will refer to people who have deliberately chosen to go live abroad on a temporary basis (e.g., usually for only a few years). They do not see themselves as immigrants because they do not want to remain in the host country; they intend to continue their journey or to return to their home country at some point. Some of them are sent by their employer and have expat contracts, but most go abroad by themselves to follow their dreams, study, or re-join a partner. We could name them expats, internationals, sojourners, or global nomads. It doesn't matter much for this book; at the psychological level, the challenges are quite similar. Just to keep things simple, the words "internationals" and "expats" will be used interchangeably.

The testimonies were collected through questionnaires, emails, workshops, and (in one case) a reader's comment posted on the Expatscience.com website. All names have been changed to maintain complete anonymity.

Fall down seven times, stand up eight times.
(nana korobi ya oki)

— Japanese Proverb

PART 1

INNER JOURNEY

Chapter 1

My Story

My big belly felt heavy, and I had a terrible back pain. As the overloaded truck travelled along the damaged Belgian highway, every jolt shook my belly and the baby we were expecting in the fall. I was keen for the eight-hour drive to finally end so that my husband and I could begin our new life in the Netherlands.

As we drew closer to the nice furnished apartment he had rented for us near his new office, I had high expectations and was satisfied that all the most important things that would ensure our smooth transition into this new culture had been set up. I had experience living in foreign cities and things had gone smoothly for me in the past, so I could not imagine there would be major problems this time. After all, I had been successful at finding a one-year contract as a researcher in a Dutch university, we were not too far away from my homeland (the Netherlands barely even felt like a foreign country), and we had just gotten married. I was not worried; I expected to settle in quickly and live a balanced life doing research and building a family.

However, this experience abroad would turn out very different from my previous two experiences. Life circumstances and timing were against me, although I didn't know it yet. I had a lot to learn still.

At the time of writing, it has been ten years since my move to the Netherlands. My experiences over those years led me to research how the scientific understanding of our emotions and cultural differences could help others make successful life transitions. In this book, I would like to share with you what I've learned about adapting to the changes of building a new life abroad and about feeling at home in a new place and among people from different cultures.

My Cultural Experience

I was not raised in a culturally diverse place. I grew up in a small village in the countryside of France, in Champagne. We were not rich, and we never travelled abroad. I left the village at eighteen to enter university in a city located 150 km away from my family, which I thought was very distant. It seemed a big leap, but my life as an international didn't truly begin until about ten years later when I moved to Brussels, Belgium, to complete my Ph.D. The move to Brussels was rather easy; people also spoke French and I had no administrative or money issues there. All I had to do was study and make new friends.

The year after that, I went to London for a post-doc. This was also a wonderful experience; I felt independent and strong, and I quickly mastered the English language and made more new friends. That year, I spent many afternoons exploring the British Museum or wandering around London. I had no family duties to stop me from doing whatever I wanted, and I had enough money to live comfortably. My intellectual life grew as well, after having learned to speak and read in English. This opened the doors to conferences and books that were not available in my native language. The whole time I was in London, I had a magnificent sense of freedom and intellectual blossoming.

Culture Shock and Helplessness

Things were very different when I tried to set up a life in the Netherlands, as I discovered only a few months after my arrival when my full-time contract was renegotiated and changed to part time. I had arrived without much knowledge of the Dutch health system, and I soon discovered that the day-care costs for our baby would equal my part-time salary, a situation that led to money issues, increased stress, and an inability to pay for more language classes or for training to get a better job.

I started to look for new jobs. In my home country, I had been a child psychologist for several years before starting to work as a researcher. Unfortunately, this was not an option in the Netherlands because my professional diploma in clinical psychology could not be validated due to language barriers. I found a few hours of work teaching here and there; however, I had long commutes to work, too little time for writing scientific papers, and little chance of getting a position as a researcher in a university because most posts were granted to locals... and on top of that, we were having couple issues. I tried everything I could think of to change this situation, but nothing seemed to work.

There were many good moments, though. I enjoyed discovering Holland and its easy-going people, making new friends in a club for young international mothers, and becoming truly fluent in English due to my contact with expats. I felt very close to my baby and spent a lot of time with him, admiring his progress at every step. My husband and I had plenty of new places to visit together on weekends – we felt like tourists, and weekends often felt like holidays. Life was good in many ways.

However, I was starting to feel extremely frustrated by my professional situation. As an expat who did not know where to get help, I started to feel like a victim of my circumstances. More and more, I was regretting the choices that had brought me into this situation. I felt stuck with too few options for building the life and career I had dreamed of. Slowly, I began to lose my confidence. I did not know what was happening to me. I thought (wrongly) that something was wrong with me. I simply did not know where to start on the road to being more efficient and happier all together.

Luckily, around this time, I learned my first important lesson about being an expat from a friend. She had lived abroad (in Australia, Asia, and Europe) for more than ten years and could speak three foreign languages. She was a true expert-expat, and she exuded confidence and optimism. She told me the following:

> *"It is really hard to be an expat, but trust me, after a while you will really like it, because you really become a much stronger person when you live abroad!"*

I remember thinking, I don't want to be stronger. All I had ever wanted was a very simple and very normal life. However, I was probably being a bit dishonest with myself, because nobody had forced me to go abroad. I had always been driven to experience and learn new things, and I hated the idea of staying in my home country and doing the same things all the time. Nevertheless, I felt that my desire for novelty was about to make me lose everything I had built.

Back in the Driving Seat of My Life

I needed to be pro-active to get out of this spiral of helplessness and get my life back under control, and learning more about psychology was the key. I started to read more about helplessness and control, stress management, cross-cultural differences, resilience theories and happiness theories. With this knowledge, and by overcoming obstacles one by one, I became ever stronger.

Every year, many people find themselves in a situation similar to the one just described. They find themselves starting over and trying to create a new life in a foreign place while facing unforeseen obstacles and unexpected difficulties. Adapting to life in a new country can rapidly become very difficult. There are important adaptive efforts that must be deployed over weeks or months before you feel right, and these constant efforts can drain your energy. There are also many frustrations and losses. Due to the many changes and the continuous need to adapt, people who settle in a foreign country typically encounter many psychological difficulties for a few months after their arrival: emotional exhaustion, stress, anxiety, depression, social dysfunction, and loss of confidence.

So how does one make the journey back to balance and independence? How does one learn to fit into a new culture and feel at home in foreign places? These questions form the basis of this book.

In my quest for explanations and solutions during my years abroad, I found many enlightening answers and helpful tips, which I have presented in the following pages in the hopes they will help you in the same way they helped me.

How to Use This Book

There is no single best way to reach a mental balance and happiness. Similarly, there is no single best way to successfully settle in a new place, feel at home or find a place in the new community. People must build their individual strengths and overcome obstacles in the ways that best fit with their life circumstances and their personality. However, based on my research in various fields, I have put together a collection of useful information and solutions that internationals can use as a framework to find direction and build on their strengths with the goal of establishing roots in a new culture.

It is not necessary to practise all the tips and exercises in this book systematically. The exercises and advice presented will affect each of us differently, and the best way to discover what works best for you is to give many different things a try. If you do not like a technique, do not believe in it, or do not feel a change, perhaps it simply does not fit your personality or your strengths. Just try several different techniques and use what works for you. It is likely that the things you like will correspond to the things you are good at, and this is where the personal change based on your strengths can happen.

If some activities suggested in the book make you feel down, worried, or discouraged, do not blame yourself and do not persist with those activities. Just try another one and use what works for you. For example, some exercises are energising while others are calming, and many people have told me they hate relaxation exercises and that these exercises just do not seem to work for them; they may even make them feel down or anxious. There is nothing wrong with you if you do not like relaxation exercises – just use what works best for you.

The overall attitude I would advise you to take is to push yourself forward into trying new behaviours and new ways of thinking, but be kind to yourself, stop if you need to, and do not criticise yourself if you fail to continue, as this would only be counter-productive.

Book Content

The first development objectives of the book focus on individual development, i.e., the abilities we can develop and practise alone. This is the focus of the chapters 2 to 5. You will learn how to build resilience, which means increasing your ability to cope with stress and life changes, feel stronger, and become a more independent, open, and flexible person. For example, you will learn techniques such as breathing to lower your general arousal level, or cognitive-therapy techniques to manage invasive thoughts such as anger.

Working on our mental representations is essential, but it is not enough. One of the major issues in expatriation is the risk of social isolation. We will address this topic in detail and explain why social isolation impacts health and why it is absolutely essential to take action to build new networks. Therefore, in chapters 6 to 9, the focus is on social life. You will learn fundamental insights to help you develop meaningful relationships with the new people you will encounter. These chapters will help you to build cross-cultural skills and learn to live in harmony with the new international environment. The objective of these chapters is to help you find a place in the new local and international communities and immerse yourself, whether through learning a new language or making new friends and building networks of acquaintances. The exercises include questions for your own self-reflection and are designed to assist you in building up your individual plan of action.

Chapter 10 puts in perspective the major challenges you may face at the psychological level during expatriation. It also lists the top ten qualities, behaviours, and ways of thinking that enable some people to cope well with difficult life changes. In the last chapter, I give a voice to the many internationals who contributed to the book through their testimonies: they talk about their learning and what they gained from the overall experience and especially from the challenges.

Chapter 2

The Arrival

— I think that becoming an expat is a real test of character and endurance.
      Simona, British, six years abroad (the Netherlands)

— I can do it. It was really hard, and I did not really know how I could survive it. I'm a lot stronger than I ever imagined. [...] I would have never grown and mature this much if I would have stayed within my own limits.
      Cintia, Portuguese, eight years abroad
(Brazil, the Netherlands, United Arab Emirates, Singapore)

— It is always a test in life to succeed in places unknown and to push yourself to your limits. The only thing I would be doing right now if I stayed at home is wondering if I had made a mistake and resenting my decision to stay home...
      Julia, Canadian, two years abroad (England, the Netherlands)

Psychological Baggage

Encountering a new culture generates changes in our identity, values, attitudes, and behaviours. John Berry, a researcher in cross-cultural psychology at Queens University in Canada who has studied cultural encounters extensively, uses the concept of acculturation to describe the changes an individual experiences as a result of being in contact with other cultures. A successful acculturation depends on individual factors, the situation, and the environment. However, what makes it a success or a never-ending spiral of issues does not depend exclusively on factors under our direct control. Before acculturation takes place, some external factors can indicate the level of difficulty that will be experienced, and many of these factors are simply there; you cannot influence them. You just have to deal with your new reality.

Cultural distance – the differences between the culture of origin and that of the host country – plays an important role. The more similar the society is to our country of origin, the easier it should be. Simple, right? Well, it is not so simple. Some expats are unpleasantly surprised to find things are much different than they expected in their newly adopted country, even when the cultures seemed similar when taken at face value. This is because cultural distance has many dimensions, some of which are deeply complex and often unexpected. These behaviours, which we will go into in more detail later, include the way managers deal with their subordinates or the way parents with their children, whether the society tolerates risk taking or is rather risk avoidant, how much importance is given to individual freedom as opposed to social cohesion, or what the society expects or values in men versus women.

Other factors matter just as much. Integrating is easier when the society promotes diversity and equality in the social structures. Life is also easier in wealthy countries, where more material comfort, more social stability, better security in general, and better health systems are available for the middle classes. Societies that expect conforming behaviours make adaptation more difficult for foreigners who do not yet know the local rules of courtesy or know what behaviours are considered acceptable and unacceptable in certain situations.

We also come into the country with ample baggage – not just great-nanny's silver forks but our mind-set, education, references, beliefs, and personality. Our personality, for example, can help or impair our adaptation. It will help a lot if you tend to be the sort of person who can tolerate ambiguity and uncertainties, be flexible and change your behaviour when faced with difficult situations, and avoid the attitude of thinking that your own ways of doing things are the best or that the local system will adapt to you.

It is useful to have the ability to take responsibility for your mistakes and learn from them instead of blaming external factors. This also requires mental flexibility. When confronted with aggressive or unfriendly behaviour, for example, it is helpful if you are able to consider whether it could be your behaviour being misinterpreted to provoke such a response (even though your behaviour might be very appropriate in the region you come from). People who tend to blame the country and its inhabitants have less drive to change their own behaviours; therefore, their ability to adapt in the future is less optimal when compared with people who can question themselves and who are ready to change.

Another personality feature that helps is being a novelty seeker. Most expats who are truly successful seek novelty in their lives, tend to be more creative and entrepreneurial than average, and tend to take risks more easily when making decisions. If you do not have this personality type – for example, if you are not an adventure seeker and you are simply accompanying a partner who drove you into this journey – you may find it more challenging to adapt and feel that you miss the stability and continuity of your old life.

Joy or Trembling after Arrival?

— I really hated it here in the first year. The very first few weeks, I loved it. It seemed like I was on an exciting vacation right at the ocean. But once that first enthusiasm wore off, I began to see everything negatively. I even had a nightmare once with the urgent feeling that I had to get us out of this country, otherwise we would not survive. [...] Each time I have moved, which was three times in the past six years, I went through exactly the same emotions. I loved it, I felt on vacation, I was thrilled to be in the new place. I then started to hate everything: the place, the people, my daily life. It was helpful to know that my emotions might be exaggerated. Especially this last move to Africa. I hated here so much that I would have packed up the next day if I had had the opportunity.

Sandra, Swiss,
six years abroad (the Netherlands, the USA, Senegal)

— The first time we moved to a new country, it was to Mexico. It was not so stressful in the beginning because there wasn't a kid yet and we still had some money, and you are in a new country enjoying that experience. We had my [Mexican] husband's family around, so it did not feel like a new country. It became more difficult when we ran out of money and had to work and move to a totally new city where we did not know anybody. I felt totally isolated from everything and everybody because my partner had to work a lot of hours and I was left alone with no car, no phone connection (so no Internet), no friends, no family; and I could not legally work there, AND I became pregnant.

Edda, Dutch,
nine years abroad
(Israel, England, Scotland, Mexico, Turkey, Greece)

Many will experience a joyful feeling in the weeks following their arrival in a new country. They may enjoy the experience because it feels like being on a long a holiday or exciting adventure. After all, most people move to a new country for good reasons. Many have landed there to take up a new job opportunity or challenge, to earn a diploma, or to re-join the love of their life. Expectations and dreams are very high, and everything seems very exciting.

However, for most expats interviewed, the expat experience was not overly positive and proved to be an unexpectedly difficult challenge from the start. According to one study, only 10% of expats have very positive feelings after arrival.

Many changes and daily domestic and administrative issues have to be faced in a short time. Just one of these would be difficult to contend with, even in a familiar place, but now we are talking about solving many issues, in a short amount of time, in an entirely new environment, while surrounded by strangers who might not speak our language. The reality is often far more complex and frustrating than we imagined.

Just like Edda and Sandra, who were very enthusiastic about travelling and very joyful at the start, most of us end up feeling more and more frustrated and unhappy once reality knocks at the door.

> — *I lived abroad from the age of nine through sixteen. I really wanted to move back overseas and become part of the international community. However, I didn't think it'd be this hard.*
> Patricia (raised in the USA, Greece, Bahrain, Holland), two years abroad (Finland)

There are big problems and big life changes to deal with such as finding or starting a new job or settling in with a partner whom we met in different circumstances. Daily life is not smooth and simple anymore. Every day brings a whole load of hassles, and, although each of them individually seems small, they accumulate rapidly and can feel overwhelming after a while.

After arriving, novelty is everywhere, even in the smallest

details, and this requires permanent adaptation. Everything takes much more time and effort than it does in a familiar place. For example, difficulties may include finding a place to live when you know neither the area nor how the local estate agents work; finding your way around; having to drive or learn to use transportation (especially difficult in a country where they use another alphabet); finding a school for your children; finding classes to learn the local language; getting things to work in the house (like the electronics you brought with you or the internet connection); finding a plumber; or finding good food (or just any food the family will find acceptable). The list goes on and on. At some point, even small things like finding a good shampoo can seem to drain a lot of energy.

All of this requires a lot of attention, and when problem solving is postponed the issues can accumulate until it all seems overwhelming. Living in a foreign place is a situation that demands constant adaptation; it may feel like there is no rest.

> — The stress mainly came from having to leave the house after the movers packed, having to be separated from my husband who had to leave earlier to Moscow, living in a hotel with two children for two weeks and working full time through the relocation. Also, the time-lines of the relocation were not clear, and it all ended up happening very quickly. [...] I was a little naive with time management and not prepared enough. I often assumed I would have time later to sort out a few things, and I did not.
>
> Gabrielle, French,
> thirteen years abroad
> (Switzerland, Russia, England, the Netherlands, Scotland)

As Gabrielle reports, as soon as the departure is programmed, life begins changing. The changes are underway even before arrival in the new country, and they will not stop in the following months.

–I do not regret our move – what is the point – but would urge people in a similar situation to think long and hard about making such a move.
Simona, British, six years abroad (the Netherlands)

A person's overall well-being and good mental health (defined as an absence of or low levels of clinical symptoms and psychosocial problems) can be described as their level of functioning. Often a person's level of functioning is severely weakened after a trauma or chronic stress (chronic stress after a move abroad is discussed in a further chapter). This drop is sometimes temporary, and the level of functioning may return to its initial level after a few weeks or months. This usually happens when the person has a good resilience and a good ability to cope with life changes. In some cases, the level of functioning ends up even higher than it was before, because the person has gained coping resources from the experience. On the other hand, a person's level of functioning could be impaired in the long term. This tends to occur when the person begins to suffer from depression.

The following figure (2.1) illustrates a hypothetical level of functioning after arrival and over the following weeks and months. Time is represented on the horizontal axis, and the level of mental functioning is represented on the vertical axis. A person's level of functioning tends to start dropping after arrival, and then different scenarios are possible: a rising slope indicates the person has the ability to cope with stressors and to feel well overall in daily life, whereas a lowering slope indicates the person is finding it more difficult to cope.

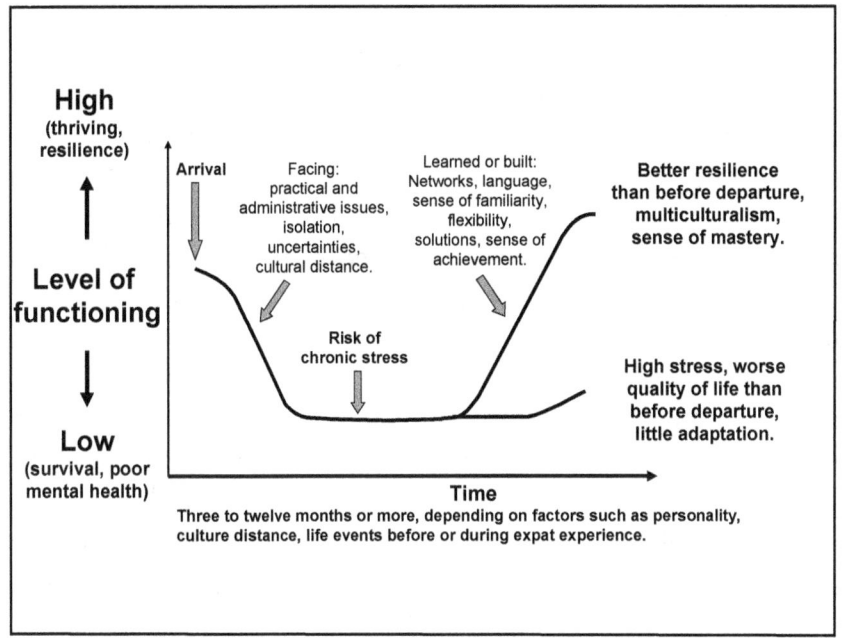

Figure 2.1. Hypothetical levels of functioning in the months following arrival in a new country.

A person's level of functioning depends upon their resiliency and ability to cope well with external stressors, as well as the number of external stressors they experience and their importance in the person's life. Most expats report a higher level of functioning (for example, they feel less worried and more flexible) after a few months or years of living abroad; their resilience levels are higher than before, and they feel they have gained a lot of inner strength from overcoming the challenges, whether alone or with their partner. However, others may settle into a state of chronic stress, suffer from homesickness, or become very negative about the experience and the host country. They may isolate themselves from the local culture. When this is the case, physical and mental health is at risk.

The curves shown in Figure 2.1 serve as a general model. For each individual, the curve will be different and may even vary over time between the two extremes (from thriving and feeling very good to succumbing and feeling depressed.).

In most cases, many stressors occur just before and just after arrival. Some expats report enjoying the first weeks, not only because of the novelty and the sense of adventure it gives them, but also because it feels good to be extremely busy. However, many stressors can continue for several weeks or in many cases for a few months, and while some practical problems may be solved during this time, many others can arise.

In addition, other major changes may occur and take up a person's limited energy. It may take weeks or months to find a job, adapt to a new work environment, visit and choose daycare or schools for children, solve Kafkaesque administrative formalities, or learn to speak the local language well enough to start having basic conversations. Besides the practical problems, the mental changes involved (for example, homesickness or acculturation issues, as addressed in the next chapters) together with the lack of family and friend support are stressful in the long term.

The time it takes for things to settle depends on the place we land, our previous experience, our preparation before departure, and our personal and professional situation (for example, settling is much easier for people travelling without family or for people who have job contracts that include financial and professional support from their company).

However, in all cases – independent of the level of local support, personal situation, or personality – it takes months before the new place starts to feel familiar and before daily routines are accompanied by a feeling of peace and safety. For the most experienced migrants, this period will take only a few weeks, but the majority report that they need between three months to one year before they find a practical routine, know where things are, and have most of their administration in place.

After this, it can still take years to learn the subtleties of the new language(s) or to adapt to deeper changes such as cultural differences in values.

Risk of Spiralling Down after Arrival

This accumulation of novelty at all levels can build up negative feelings such as frustration, sadness, disappointment, rage, the sense that life is unfair, jealousy towards those who seem to have an easy life, and antipathy towards locals. Scientific studies observing the adaptation of international students, expats, and immigrants to their life abroad have shown that levels of depression are highest during the first month or months after arrival: their feelings are quite negative towards the entire experience and towards the host country to start with but become more positive after four months to one year, depending on the individual and their circumstances. In studies observing Japanese, Malaysian, and Singaporean students arriving in New Zealand, and in Chinese scholars arriving in Canada, levels of depression and anxiety were still higher than they were before departure even six months after their arrival in the new country.

While there is a lot of individual variation, overall a surprisingly large number of people will experience depression, anxiety disorders, low levels of psychological well-being, and other mental health problems that they were not experiencing before departure. In the studies mentioned, the increase in negative feelings happened in more than half of the people interviewed, and a small proportion reached the level of clinical depression, meaning that the symptoms became so overwhelming that professional assistance was necessary.

For the other interviewees, the most resilient ones, a time of habituation was still necessary but their positive experiences were stronger than the negative ones. The move to another country was perceived as an interesting challenge but not as excessively difficult.

In most cases, even for those who found it very difficult at the start, things progressively get better: one by one, each problem is solved, cultural differences start to feel familiar and laughable, and friends are found to share sorrows with, go out with, or consult for information. (In Figure 2.1, this is the point where the slope starts to rise rapidly after a long low period). Stressors disappear one after another, but something else changes too: expats report that they feel stronger and proud to have overcome the earlier obstacles.

> — *[The main challenge is] to learn to live all alone and to cope with difficulties with no help from others. [...] I learned to deal with problems and stress, and I think I make less "fuss" about everything difficult.*
>
> Tijana, Serbian,
> three years abroad (Hungary, the Netherlands)

For most of us, the increase in resilience and the diminishing level of stress does not take place quickly, and for a minority it does not take place at all. You may hear them (or is it perhaps you?) complaining endlessly about their host country. When I spoke to Tania, a woman from the Middle East who spent eleven months in the Netherlands, she gave me an endless list of complaints: the people there are absolutely cold and unwelcoming, the children are not even alive, the food is so tasteless a dog would get depressed by it, their TV news is useless, there is no beauty in the landscape... and such bad weather... racist neighbours... ignorant doctors... dangerous stairs.... I tried to say something nice about the country and its people, but my comments only seemed to make her more negative; she wanted to go back home.

This type of negative discourse is not unusual in people who have just arrived in a new country, wherever it is. It is usual to hear their lists of complaints and frustrations at international parties and meet-up events or to see their negative comments on web forums. This negativity is triggered by the initial culture shock.

Experienced internationals tend to smile and think, Yeah, yeah, I've been there; I know. With experience, criticisms soften and usually leave in their place a relaxed attitude, an appreciation of new ways of doing things, laughter about awkward situations, and the reflex action of wanting to help each other and share good tips and useful addresses rather than complain about things that cannot be changed.

Tania's words alarmed me because she had been in the country for almost a year. Usually, after a year, people have become used to how things are done and start to appreciate and learn from the cultural differences. Individuals who struggle to understand and accept their new environment may find their level of functioning does not go up, and they will either need a lot of support to remain or they may have to leave in order to remain mentally healthy and regain emotional balance.

Sense of Helplessness and Losing Control

Moving abroad and having few resources to change your situation can lead to a feeling of helplessness. For example, if you follow your husband or wife to support your spouse's positive career move, you may suddenly feel you have little control over your life. You may not have the legal permission to work in the country or may not be able to find as secure a job as you had back home. You may realize that your diplomas will not help you to find a job at all or find that, despite being considered as highly skilled in your own country, you feel worthless in the new place. You can become financially dependent on your spouses for the first time and feel diminished and weakened by the situation. You may have the sense you are losing your identity and feel helpless about it.

The terrible effects of helplessness and loss of self-confidence on physical and mental health have been observed by Bob Rose in a large-scale study involving US air traffic controllers. Air traffic controllers have very demanding jobs because they must pay attention to complex information for hours, and inattention and mistakes can cost lives. During a conflict between the employers and the unions, Robert Rose was asked to explore whether the working conditions might explain the higher-than-average incidence of health issues (some of them were developing high blood pressure as early as age thirty).

With his colleagues, Rose observed their psychological and physical conditions at the time of the conflict. Twenty years later, he was able to find the participants of the study and test them again. By age fifty, a number of them had developed heart disease, high blood pressure, alcoholism, or depression with a higher incidence than the average population. A powerful finding was that the psychological factors measured when they were thirty years old had a bigger impact on their chance of developing diseases at fifty than other body-health indicators (for example, blood pressure). In fact, feeling a sense of alienation and abandonment at thirty was found to predict whether they would experience depression and anxiety twenty years later.

This study, among others that corroborate this conclusion, illustrates how feeling a lack of control over one's life influences physical and mental health: when you feel you lack control, a situation can seem far more stressful than if you were experienced and prepared. In order to feel better, you need to feel (and be) in control. Getting your life back under your own control is important. In the long term, it also helps you build a strong identity that does not depend upon your geographic location, job, or partner.

There is at least one thing you can always control under all circumstances: the way you think. By changing your ways of thinking, you can put yourself into a more optimistic mode, have more impact on your environment, and avoid experiencing a feeling of helplessness. Overcoming your sense of being stuck without options is an early step towards helping you change your situation and create a life that is more exciting and fun than your current one.

Obstacles Are Also Opportunities

When confronted with a new problematic situation, a cascade of reactions takes place in our thoughts. Similar events can play out differently for different people, depending on our anticipation of the situation, current mind-set, personality, and the context of the problem. Figure 2.2 is a schematic representation of the cognitive appraisal of a new situation and its consequences on our behaviours, thoughts, and, ultimately, body functions.

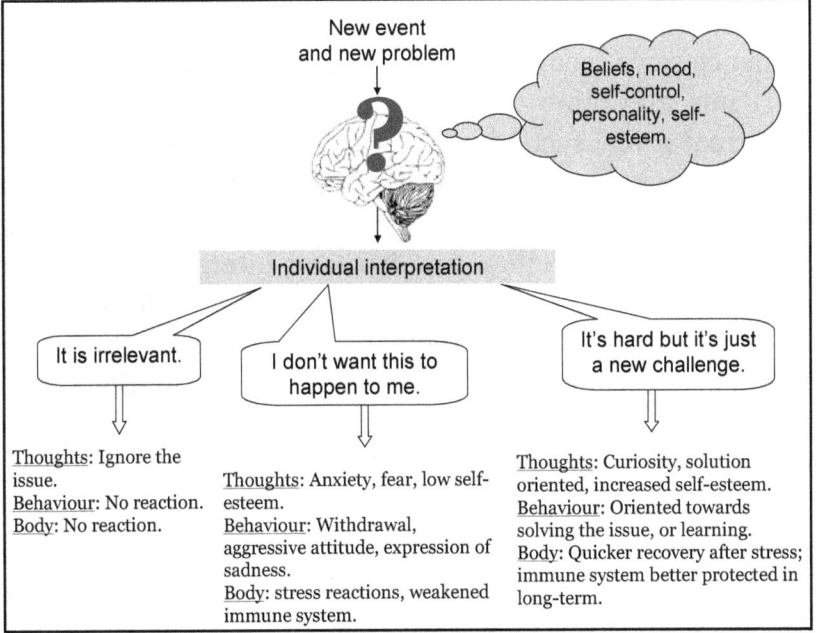

Figure 2.2. The meaning of a new event depends on the person who interprets it.

The cognitive appraisal of the same situation varies in different people. Faced with a new situation, some will not think much about it, some will have strong negative feelings about it, and others will express very positive feelings.

Experimental studies indicate that the cognitive appraisal of a stressful situation is key to understanding why some people present a better recovery after a stressful event. Michele Tugade and Barbara Frederickson observed how people react to stress and discovered some particular ways the most resilient ones seem to think about stressful situations. They recruited university students for their study and scored their resilience levels with a questionnaire built by two resilience specialists, John Block and Adam Kremen. They presented the students with situations that generated anxiety: they told the participants to get ready to give a presentation in front of other people. In such situations, people react and experience changes in their heart rate and blood pressure.

The authors noticed that students scoring high on the resilience scale recovered more quickly than others did: their heart rate and other body measures of stress bounced back to normal a few seconds after the stress was over, while in others it took about one minute. The resilient students also expressed more positive feelings toward the task than the other students did; they saw it as an interesting challenge to take on, and they did not complain, react with distress or act as victims. Curiously, their markers of stress during the experience were similar to the other students' markers. They experienced similar stress during the task but simply had a much quicker recovery afterwards.

That is not the end of the story; it gets more interesting: the same researchers discovered that it was possible to change students' thoughts and help them to become more resilient just by suggesting to them beforehand that they would take positive rewards from this situation. Students were told, for example, to consider the situation as an interesting challenge from which they would learn something interesting.

This is very important because stressful situations always contain some positive aspects: at the least, they enable us to learn about the environment or to learn something about ourselves. Sometimes we have to overcome hurdles to reach long-term and highly important goals in life. If you appraise the situation as something that serves a purpose, or if you are sure you are getting something out of it, then you will feel in control of your destiny rather than feel you are a victim of random and disagreeable events. See how the three persons below reacted to their transition to a new life abroad and to some difficult life events that occurred several years after their move.

> — In the Netherlands, I experienced [culture shock and negative feelings] in full, with diagnosed severe depression and an outbreak of autoimmune disease. I became a client of "psychosomatiek" department for a time. I refused to go out of the house and have any human contacts, even at the shop. The worst experience were the contacts with immigration service and local lawyers who pretended to "work on my issue" but in fact lied and pulled out money month after month. Since then, I have learned not to trust any counselling and to read the laws myself. There were awful local hospitals and doctors [...]. We have a house of our own, considered a "nice one," but it is rather my husband's home, his dream place, than mine. I hate countryside. I hate having to go by car do my shopping. I hate garbage collected once a week only. [...] It is a quest for survival rather than a road to home.
> Tatiana, Russian,
> five years abroad (Germany, the Netherlands)

> — It is a prisoner island here; historically it was, and it still is! I have to stay for my child. But I feel like a prisoner here. In a few years, I'll return home to Canada, when my daughter is old enough to follow me.
> Thomas, Canadian,
> ten years abroad (Australia)

> — My true home will always be Ireland, where my extended family is; however, I have no intention of moving there. My home away from home for now is Delft, Netherlands. I have a house that I can work on to build it into a home. [...] For the previous five years in the US, I was already remote from family and was living in a relatively small town. I was eager to get out and explore a new location. I consider myself an independent person who can handle/enjoy periods of isolation. When this feeling was high, I would try a new sport/club, get out to meet people, anything I could do to keep busy. [...] I am happier now than I would be if I had stayed in the U.S. I found that I was never meant to be in small-town USA. Making that decision to leave was not easy, but I do not regret the decision. It encourages me to follow my instincts.
>
> Mike,
> raised in England, Ireland, and five states in the USA,
> five years abroad as an adult (the USA, the Netherlands)

Why do some of us adapt successfully, find ways to cope in the new place, start to enjoy the new lifestyle, and then accept or decide that there will probably be no return ticket, while others suffer as if living in hell, feel like prisoners, and hate most things in their new place? What helps?

There are many factors we do not control, as evidenced in the examples above: life circumstances were difficult for Tatiana and Thomas. Thomas chose to stay in a foreign country in order to remain with his child following a divorce and shared-custody arrangement. Tatiana became sick and suffered from a weak immune system, which is associated with poor resistance to stress. This could explain her difficulties with coping.

On the other hand, Mike could also have complained and felt very bad about being so far from his "home," but instead he made decisions that allowed him to adapt to new situations successfully: he actively sought company when he was feeling lonely; he shifted his priorities in life; and he changed his ways of relating to people. He now lives with a girlfriend, and they are renovating a house they bought. He does not say it was easy, but he has gained self-confidence in his private life and, despite working less, he thinks he has gained more than if he had not moved. He is clearly very pro-active in his way of thinking and tends to see the positive side and take the best out of each situation. Note that he also had previous experience with moving abroad, so he probably developed flexibility and resilience from an early age.

Both Tatiana and Thomas have something in common: they see themselves as victims of a situation where many things seem to have been decided by others (her husband's house; his divorce). This makes it very hard for them to cope, and they feel out of control. This increases their stress and negative feelings and leaves them no room to find solutions, because the only solution they see is to get their former lives back. They only see what they regret and what they have lost, not what their new life and future could look like or how they could use their new circumstances to build new dreams. Thomas and Tatiana both reject their host countries; they hate being there and both avoid embracing the culture or being influenced by it, and they also avoid finding friends or making long-term relationships. Tatiana says she will not make friends nor even talk with the people around her, and Thomas says that he does not want to date women in Australia because he does not want to develop bonds to the country.

Both of them suffer a lot. Tatiana is clearly depressed and diagnosed as such, and Thomas regularly gets drunk to forget his unhappiness and isolation. Because they feel stuck, they seem to live in the present and are not able to think much further ahead.

In contrast, Mike's pro-active way of thinking certainly helps him focus on problem solving. He sees the changes that happened to him as events that taught him something. There are things he misses, but he also values what he gained from the changes.

Pro-active thinking and the positive appraisal of stressful situations not only helps us to feel good but also helps significantly in terms of finding solutions to problems, even in situations that look hopeless. The following text describes a systematic method that can help you to react pro-actively and build more optimism and psychological strength when faced with a difficult situation.

Cognitive Technique: The ABCDE (Ellis)

Cognitive techniques can alleviate or soften negative feelings such as helplessness, low self-esteem, anger, or regret. The feelings might not completely disappear, but they will become less intrusive and less painful. The objective is to stop feeling anxious when you experience these feelings by developing new mental habits and constructive ways of thinking that will replace automatic thoughts of sadness or procrastination.

As a foreigner, you may feel trapped, misunderstood, isolated, lonely, angry, threatened by xenophobic comments, frustrated, tired of speaking a foreign language with a strong accent, distressed by the perspective of a blocked career, or very anxious about the future.

Such feelings are understandable, and they are a normal reaction to situations that are, indeed, very difficult. A foreigner feels less competent than locals do in many domains due to lack of knowledge or language barriers, and sometimes because of discrimination. You may be a world expert in your field, you may speak six languages, you may have been crowned the mum of the year in your city, or perhaps you used to know everybody in your neighbourhood... but when you arrive in a new country, you suddenly feel you are a nobody who cannot do even the most simple things. Consequently, you may start to think you are incompetent in other domains as well.

Cognitive techniques can help alleviate this sense of helplessness and provide you with the mental space to think creatively about solutions. The ABCDE exercise (next page) is a classic in cognitive-behavioural therapy. It became a standard because it works so well, and it is especially recommended when dealing with very intrusive and repetitive thoughts. For example, it has been used successfully to help depressed people or people with obsessive thoughts (feelings or ideas that seem to be present all the time and cannot be easily stopped).

This technique, pioneered by psychologist Albert Ellis, originated as the ABC technique. The longer version, the ABCDE technique, is intended to train the participant to become aware of their thoughts and of when they occur. The person must then challenge these thoughts, stop them each time they occur, become critical of them, and replace them with positive thoughts.

This exercise is very powerful despite its apparent simplicity. If you practise it several times, it becomes a mental habit that will come to the rescue in many situations (in the Appendix, you can find the ABCDE exercise to photocopy and use whenever necessary). This exercise teaches you how to avoid being overwhelmed and dominated by automatic ways of thinking that are harmful or not constructive. It also provides you with more freedom in the long-term, because it forces you to become aware of more choices in terms of how you can react. Becoming mentally flexible is an outcome of this exercise: it trains you to see the same situation from different perspectives and to challenge your first impressions.

Many expats thank their life abroad for enabling them to develop the necessary quality of mental flexibility. Their transition into the new situation demanded that they become an expert at finding new ways of thinking, behaving, interpreting ambiguous situations, and finding new solutions.

ABCDE TECHNIQUE

This exercise (adapted from A. Ellis & J. Harper, *A Guide to Rational Living*, 2001) helps diminish negative ideas and boost pro-activity.

A series of five questions guides you through trying to figure out an alternative interpretation and a new solution to your problem. Instead of feeling trapped, bad, or guilty, you will build a pro-active approach.

The exercise is not meant to distort reality and convince you that you should think differently. This would not work. Just try your best to think about alternative interpretations that you believe in.

A. ADVERSITY: Write down a problem you are facing, and describe what you find really annoying, painful, frustrating about this situation.

Example: *None of my colleagues ever invites me for a drink after work, and they declined my invitations as well. I have very few friends here. I'd like to be friends with some of my colleagues, but this is not happening.*

B. BELIEF: What do you think your negative beliefs about this problem are? What is your interpretation of the situation? What negative generalizations does this problem generate or support?

Example: *People are very unfriendly in this country (general negative statement about host culture). Perhaps I am not good at making friends after all; perhaps I am not a good person (lowering self-esteem).*

C. CONSEQUENCE: Describe how you are feeling and how you are acting as a consequence of this belief.

Example: *I feel terribly lonely. I feel like I must be doing some things wrong, otherwise people would invite me. They seem polite, but perhaps it is only a professional attitude and not sincere. They do not seem to like me or even know who I really am. I gave up on inviting anybody after trying several times.*

D. DISPUTE: Think about other possible interpretations. In particular, imagine the point of view of the other persons, and the cultural differences.

Example: No one said anything negative about me and people are friendly with me during working hours, so there is no evidence that I did something wrong or that they do not like me. I have had many friends in the past, so there is nothing wrong with me. I am not asocial; on the contrary, I am a friendly person in the culture I come from.

E. ENERGIZE: Consider more optimistic explanations for your problem so that it energizes you, lifts your spirit, and so you become more hopeful, less anxious. Then take appropriate action. If it does not work at first, try again in a different way.

Example: Perhaps they did not understand how it was for me because it is not in the tradition here to go out for a drink with colleagues immediately after work. So there must be other cultural ways colleagues socialize. I have to discover them. I can talk about this with locals; I can find more information on the social habits of the local people on books or websites. I can ask other expats how they deal with this. Once I know the local habits better, I will change my style and invite/see people in a more culturally appropriate way. If they refuse my invitation, I will not give up, but I will talk about my desire to make more friends and about my own cultural references and ask them about their customs.

If you practise this exercise several times, you will take the habit of seeing alternative interpretations. This will open your eyes to other ways to look at the same situation, find new solutions, and take more appropriate actions when facing issues.

Optimism or Pessimism?

Martin Seligman, a specialist of positive psychology, has studied both the mechanisms underlying optimism and pessimism and the performance of optimists as compared to pessimists. He concluded that, overall, it is better to be optimistic because it enables us to take more risks, recover quicker from mistakes, and achieve more.

The exception to this rule is when large risks are involved, for example, when lives are on the line. We would not want an airplane pilot or a surgeon to neglect a procedure or safety rule. In high-risk situations, it is necessary to remain pessimistic and to think ahead about everything that could go wrong.

Expatriation and repatriation are major life decisions because they can jeopardise a career, put in peril a family's financial or emotional stability, or compromise family members' health and well-being. It is better to anticipate all the possibilities, expect that something could go wrong, manage the risks and have a back-up plan. It is also better to be aware that difficult moments are a natural consequence of the adaptation process.

An important factor in coping with life changes is to manage your expectations. The principle is, it is better to have low expectations at the start (one aspect of pessimism) because this helps you anticipate the changes that are coming, including the negative events. Having too high expectations puts you at risk of not being prepared to face hurdles and obstacles.

Unexpected difficulties are more damaging than difficulties you have already thought about, and this is why some worrying is beneficial –provided it is within realistic limits. A little bit of pessimism is safer. Anticipating stress and hurdles (for example, what will happen if your spouse cannot get a work permit) prepares you, because you can think about what to do ahead of time. Both before and during your stay in a foreign country, it is important to prepare plan-B alternatives in case particular objectives cannot be reached. As a friend of mine told me recently, only half-joking, "My husband and I, we discuss regularly our plans for the future, where we will go next. We have many scenarios in mind. We have a plan B, but we also have Plans C, D and E, F!"

People who return to their home country after expatriation often have overly optimistic expectations for their return. With distance, and after not having lived a real life in their home country for years, they tend to romanticize their country, only remembering the best parts of their life at home. Memories can become extremely distorted. Much research in psychology and economics suggests that we tend to remember moments of intense emotions far more readily than the daily aspects and repetitive tasks of an ordinary life, even though the not-so-exciting moments are what most of life is made of. This is what leads us to romanticize our past.

People who think about repatriation should anticipate arriving in a place that has changed a lot, where the people they knew might have moved away, changed, turned a page, or simply be too busy to spend much time with newcomers. They will also have to go through all the usual administrative hurdles, just as they just did in the foreign country.

The overall lesson is, before departure and before repatriation, be prepared. When I arrived in the Netherlands, I came with expectations that were not adequate. My biggest mistake concerned the childcare system. I thought that Northern Europe in general was a great place for working women, and I believed the stereotype that women were treated as equal to men. I expected a very advanced social system and easily available day-care for working mums.

I was totally wrong. Although the Netherlands is a wonderful country for children to live in, day-care is suboptimal: it is expensive and the waiting lists are huge. Most women with small children simply stop working or work part time because the cost of day care is almost equal to their salary, and many men work part time to share the childcare with their partner. In the Netherlands, 50% percent of all women do not work (compared with only 20% in my home country).

I had no idea and ended up very distressed by the difficulties I faced in finding day-care. My unfulfilled expectations created a sense of lack of control that was damaging in the long term. Because the difficulties continued for months, I started to think I had done something wrong or had missed some hidden solutions. In retrospect, I know that I could not find what was wrong because there was nothing wrong... except my expectations. However, because of my wrong assumptions at the time and the lack of quick solutions, I started to blame myself and lose my self-confidence. The problem of losing self-confidence is not only about the worsening of disagreeable feelings; it also drains our energy and makes it more difficult to find solutions to our problems.

The conclusion as to whether a pessimistic or optimistic attitude is better when moving abroad could be this: While having a pessimistic attitude helps in making wise decisions, we benefit from being optimistic once we have made our decisions and are facing our first obstacles. Optimism helps us to find creative solutions and it sustains our motivation to pursue our goals, thus transforming obstacles into challenges.

Keep a Record of Your Progress

Systematically writing down your fears and worries and reflecting on them reduces them by allowing you to take a critical look at your own ways of thinking. Writing and reflection has been shown to reduce anxiety and boost performance. It is not procrastination, and it will not exacerbate your painful emotions; rumination tends to be decreased in depressed people who reflect on their own written thoughts.

Keeping a written record is also an efficient way to progress and to monitor your progress. You could, for example, write down ideas as you read this book and then use this list to take actions that will increase your well-being. Also consider writing down the thoughts that come to your mind while practicing some of the exercises, such as the ABCDE exercise.

When you make writing a habit, you become more aware of your own thoughts and discover the power you have to develop more constructive thoughts and to evoke them when necessary in many situations. In the long term, it enlarges your aptitude to feel and practise both compassion and openness to others, two abilities that are critical to adjusting successfully to international environments, as we will see in Part 2.

Habitual writing will also help you remain motivated to keep learning and exploring yourself and your new environment: read your diary entries after a few days or a few weeks, and you will be surprised to see how fast you can change and build inner strength and wisdom.

Chapter 3

Loneliness

A large majority of the expats I interviewed declared that they felt very lonely at times and suffered from loneliness more in their new country than their own country. Many said they felt lonely more often, although most had learned – with varying degrees of success – to cope with it. Some were able to cope well and found creative ways to fill in the empty hours, for example, by learning to paint or writing novels, but that was only a minority of the interviewees.

> — I'm very lucky that I have my husband, but, apart from that, I have made almost no friends in the Netherlands apart from a few very nice colleagues.[...] I did feel lonely and regretted not having any close female friends around. I found that my salvation was in my work, which kept me very busy and did not allow me time to mope!
>
> Simona, British,
> six years abroad (the Netherlands)

— I had three friends I could talk to about serious matters, but two have moved in the last year. [...] Yes, I'm lonely. I tried to join clubs and go to expat groups to alleviate this feeling, but I take a long time to feel comfortable with people, and I'm very busy with my family and work. The one group I've connected with is my book club since I'm passionate about reading and writing.

Sarah, US citizen,
four years abroad (Ireland, the Netherlands)

— Yes, I suffered from loneliness when I saw my close friends leave. Also when I was ill, far from my family who could have taken care of my children or my house. Even though the local people helped, it is not the same. I also felt very lonely with my illness (I had a cancer). At home, I could have joined support groups, called support centres. But not here, and this was really hard. If it had happened later, I could have managed it differently. Now I am more centred on my family, I am more "armoured" and I have less need of others. So I do not suffer from loneliness any longer.

Christine, French,
twelve years abroad (the Netherlands)

Loneliness and Separation

Loneliness is a form of fear and pain associated with a particular situation, such as chronic social isolation or sudden separation. It is something rooted in our bodily make-up. We are genetically programmed to be a gregarious species: we are meant to live with other people around us, become attached to them, and share intimacy and love with them in various forms. We are meant to be part of a group and have a role in this group.

Look at how a baby reacts to isolation in a matter of seconds. When a mother is asked by a researcher to stay still and not react to her baby's smiles for several seconds, the baby quite rapidly starts to show signs of distress: the baby becomes agitated and starts to cry for attention. If the experiment continues for a few more minutes, the baby withdraws and becomes very lethargic. At this point, the experiment has to stop.

When young children are raised in orphanages where little warmth and no individual care is provided due to ignorance or lack of resources (for example, in the former Yugoslavia in the '90s), or when hospitalized children are left on their own for long periods of time and their psychological needs are not taken care of (for example, the way the polio disease was treated in early twentieth century by leaving children in artificial lungs for months), severe and irreversible mental disorders are observed. Receiving love and parental care from an early age is not only nice; it is one of our most fundamental psychological needs.

This continues to some extent throughout adulthood. Isolation is one of the ultimate punishments in many communities, and it takes many forms, from shame and ostracism to containment cells in prisons. Social isolation for a long period is a very painful experience. The loss of someone beloved, a break-up after a romantic love affair, or a divorce are among the most painful and distressing life events in all cultures, at all ages, for men and women alike. These events are followed by a sense of emptiness that is difficult to describe in words. This intense pain has been a source of inspiration for artists, poets, and musicians for thousands of years, and it is reported in all societies.

Loneliness is probably associated with the terrors of being left alone and abandoned in our very early lives. This fear might have evolved in our species because being alone would have been dangerous for the young, so our brain evolved to be particularly sensitive to this.

The Chemistry of Loneliness

The mechanisms underlying feelings of loneliness are not fully understood, but some of the chemical pathways that underlie attachment between humans have been identified. They are universal among humans and can be found in other mammals as well. A century ago, the protein oxytocin was discovered by Henry Dale. It is produced by the pituitary gland (which has also a role in the stress reaction). Oxytocin plays a role in pacing the birth process and is likely to be involved (as part of a complex hormonal reaction) in the attachment found between mothers and their newborns. It is found in higher concentrations in the blood of very social animal species than it is in nonsocial species.

In humans, oxytocin is found in higher concentrations in people experiencing romantic relationships, and it is also higher after sexual intercourse. Oxytocin seems to play a leading role in attachment and positive social relationships between parents and children and between lovers, but also to some extent in other social relationships and soothing situations. For example, a study found oxytocin levels were raised during a massage.

The chemistry of social bonding and its pathways in the brain are still being investigated by the new scientific field of social neuroscience: a science where a lot remains to be discovered. There is more than one chemical involved, and the mechanisms involved are extremely complex, but scientists are progressing rapidly towards an understanding of the chemistry of social relationships.

When Loneliness Becomes Chronic

The facts presented so far should convince you that there is nothing unusual in feeling lonely, and you are perfectly normal if you experience loneliness. It is just a signal telling you to increase your social bonds in quality and quantity. This signal is sent to your brain when the soothing roles of social bonds are lacking. So, if you feel temporarily lonely from time to time, there is nothing wrong with you; it is a healthy signal.

The problem is that loneliness can become a chronic condition. When you experience loneliness very often, cry a lot and get disheartened by it on a regular basis, or when it is associated with strong anxiety every day, this is not a healthy signal anymore, and your mental balance and physical health start to be impaired.

The devastating effects of social isolation and chronic loneliness (the feeling of being left alone, even when in reality you have some good social connections) have been the focus of many epidemiological studies in recent decades. The negative effects of isolation on health and mortality can be compared to the negative impact that a lack of physical exercise or smoking has on physical health. For example, in both men and women, the mortality rate in the year following the loss of their spouse is much higher than it is in the average population. In people with similar numbers of social relationships, those who feel lonely often experience poorer health outcomes when compared to people who do not experience this feeling often.

Individual Reactions to Solitude and Isolation

— *I decided to prioritise making friends over other things (like learning the language) and therefore made some good friends pretty quickly. The only way in which I felt isolated was that there was nobody from my particular country in the group (whereas there seemed to be at minimum two people from all of the other countries).*

Gaby, Australian,
four years abroad (the Netherlands, England)

— *I did feel lonely at the start, but this was mainly because I was living in a guest house with a couple of Danish people, a bunch of Japanese people and... me... the only Dutch. Understandably, the inter-internationals spent more time with each other, spoke their own language and undertook things as a group, and I was more or less the "outstander." To overcome this feeling, I started to go out on my own, open-minded, to meet people.*

Karen, Dutch,
six months abroad (Uganda)

— *In the place I live in now, I only have my husband to talk to about serious problems. I have to call my very close friends who live in other parts of the world when I want to discuss serious problems with someone else. I miss having very close friends nearby. [...] I am not very good at making new friends, as I am not very outgoing. After each move, it took me about a year to feel like I had some friends.*
So I started to explore new hobbies. I started to get into yoga, my own art projects and I wrote a novel. I think I would never have started painting and writing if I had stayed in my home country. As art and writing are very important aspects of who I am now, I'm glad that I moved to find that out. [...] In general, I believe I am more open to new experiences and unconventional

friendships because I am alone and out of my own society. I believe moving abroad not only opens your horizon in regard to the world but also in regard to yourself.

Sandra, Swiss,
six years abroad (the Netherlands, the USA, Senegal)

Some people can cope very well with solitude; they can tolerate moving away from their family and friends without much distress. Even with very few friends around them, they will not report loneliness and distress. Solitude enables them to be more independent, and they enjoy having room to be themselves without much external pressure. Some among us have chosen professions or hobbies that require long periods of isolation. Artists, writers, artisans, or researchers, for example, have to spend long periods in solitude to focus on their art and develop creativity.

However, many people need immersion in close social experiences in order to feel balanced and good. For them, there is a risk of downward spiralling and developing a self-defeating attitude when confronted with the challenge of moving abroad and having to start a new life with very little social support.

The level at which we can tolerate loneliness results from complex early interactions between our genetic heritage and our early experiences in life. John Cacioppo, a specialist of loneliness, describes a "genetic thermostat" of loneliness (or of perceived social isolation): we all experience loneliness on some days, but the genetic lottery and early experiences make some of us more sensitive or more resilient than others. Loneliness is less strong when our caregivers responded flexibly and adequately to our attachment needs when we were infants and toddlers. It is also influenced by early life events, such as traumatic separations during very early childhood.

Some authors argue that a person's attachment style, which

greatly influences our ability to cope with situations and affects self-confidence and autonomy, is not totally fixed. There is room for change even during adulthood. In a remarkable case study, Daniel Siegel, a psychotherapist for children and adults who specialises in attachment and early traumas, describes a man whose relationships with others, including his wife, were very distant for most of his life. Following a life crisis, he entered into psychotherapy and as a result saw his ability to connect emotionally improve dramatically – at the age of ninety. Siegel concludes that it is never too late to change.

It is noteworthy that Siegel uses relaxation techniques to increase body-mind awareness and to reinstall health and a strong awareness of emotional reactions. This awakening of our emotions does not lead to more suffering; on the contrary, it improves health.

Loneliness and Raising Emotional Awareness

The body sensations generated by loneliness reach our mind (we become aware of them) and generate painful feelings. Reconnecting the body and mind enables us to diminish the intensity of the fear and pain associated with loneliness.

Joseph Ledoux is a specialist of emotions and, in particular, of fear. In his book *The Emotional Brain*, he describes the relationships between the body, brain, and mind, and explains how fears and other emotions are generated. Fear is a very important emotion because it is present in various mental states, although we are not necessarily aware of this. There are components of fear in feelings such as loneliness, anxiety, and probably also in anger and depression.

Before reaching the brain centres responsible for our awareness, fear affects the body. After perceiving danger (via the eyes, ears, or nose), signals are sent to the brain to alert the centres that specialise in reacting to fearful stimuli (including the amygdala), activating a cascade of reactions. The autonomic nervous system (the extremely complex network of nerves that controls our heart rate, blood pressure, sweat glands, etc.) activates a fight, flight, or freeze response, which in turn causes body reactions at the muscular level and internal-organ level.

The vital parts of our brain – those that maintain our lives – are located in the deeper and lower parts of our brain. They protect us every second, doing the underground jobs we do not need to consciously think about: regulating body temperature and heart rate, controlling breathing, and enabling us to fall asleep when needed.

By contrast, our consciousness makes us aware of only a very small part of what happens inside us. The parts of our brains involved in processing consciousness are in specific frontal areas (the orbital cortex, and the anterior cingulated cortex). When signals from internal organs are sent to the upper parts of our brain (for example, fast heartbeats, short and rapid breaths, and very tense muscles), we consciously experience a change but have to use our understanding of the situation to interpret the internal change (e.g. we may say, "I feel afraid," "I feel unwell," "I am so anxious," or "I do not want to do this.") Feelings are the by-product of this loop between body and brain. Feelings reach our awareness because they are built by our brains in the "thinking" areas: the frontal lobes. They can be remembered and we can reflect on them.

In fact, we are mostly only aware of what happens externally – what we see, hear, taste, touch, or smell – and we pay little attention to the signals sent to our consciousness by our internal organs. This is why emotions and feelings are sometimes so confusing. We are often puzzled about feeling the way we do and cannot always explain how we feel or why.

Learning to control and deal with feelings starts with increasing our awareness of our own body signals. In other words, we must reconnect the body and the mind. From there, we can learn to cope progressively better with these feelings, feel less overwhelmed, and prevent them from becoming chronic and invading our daily lives.

The techniques of focus and relaxation (or mindfulness) as they have been developed in the Western and Eastern relaxation techniques such as meditation and yoga engage the attention networks and allow us control of our emotions so that we may reduce stress. Experimental studies show that by practising meditation or relaxation techniques on a daily basis (even if only for a few minutes a day) for a few weeks, people's general feeling of well-being and their ability to control themselves and their emotions is significantly improved. We will see how in the next chapter. First, let's see why loneliness is so distressing and learn what to do to prevent chronic loneliness.

How Lonely People Isolate Themselves Further

The typical lonely person is one who seems sarcastic, withdrawn or does not have fun during outings. For example, they will complain a lot, not smile much, not seem interested in others (because they are too absorbed in their own pain), and may yell at their partner or accuse them of not caring. In a marriage, the lonely partner can start to complain that the other person is not fulfilling their need for affection, while the other partner (who may have less need for connectedness) sees the complaining partner as too difficult and too demanding. This starts to pull partners apart and increases the feelings of loneliness and associated unhappiness.

Experimental studies conducted in young students and in ageing populations suggest that lonely persons perceive the social signals around them more acutely than non-lonely people; however, their problem lies in their interpretation of the social signals. When feeling lonely, we feel less fulfilled by our interactions with people, even when we spend time with a friend or a person who is agreeable and emotionally supportive. As a result, we benefit less from the positive impact of everyday interactions. Such behaviour is very counterproductive because a connection with someone normally brings us joy, fun and comfort, and thus relief from the loneliness.

This was also shown in a brain-imaging study where happy faces activated the reward areas of the brain to a lesser extent in people feeling lonely than it did in a sample of comparable people with low scores of loneliness.

Being aware of this bias is a starting point that can help you decide to open your eyes to other ways of seeing reality and also to take responsibility for your feelings of loneliness. It also helps show why adopting a victim position is very counterproductive. However, effecting this change is very difficult because feelings of loneliness are usually accompanied by sadness and self-depreciation.

Reduce Feelings of Loneliness and Social Isolation

> — I'm a social person by nature and seem to find people everywhere.... And being lonely feels good at times – nothing wrong with that.
>
> Cintia, Portuguese,
> eight years abroad (Brazil, the Netherlands,
> the United Arab Emirates, and Singapore)

Of course, building relationships with others and reducing social isolation is essential to reducing feelings of loneliness. When arriving in a new country, it is crucial to rapidly build a new network of acquaintances and friends. The hurdles to this process will be addressed in the following chapters. In reading these chapters, you will have many opportunities to reflect on your own cultural biases and see how they affect your relationships, and also to reflect on your networks and find ways to build stronger and larger networks of acquaintances and friends.

But we have seen that loneliness is also a state of mind that, as such, needs to be addressed at the individual level. Loneliness distorts our social cognition because our perceptions and expectations are influenced by our emotional states of unhappiness and fear. Changing our perceptual biases helps us to feel more confident about building new relationships or improving on existing ones. It is a sort of mental fitness; it helps us to maintain good mental health in the long term. You can learn to cope with, and ultimately even appreciate, your moments of solitude.

The ABCDE technique can help people who feel isolated by changing their interpretations (Chapter 2). Relaxation and visualisation techniques, such as the focus technique presented in detail in the next chapter, will also prove very helpful. The objective of relaxation is to develop a better ability to regulate anxiety, fear, body reactions, and tension. It helps to become aware of your own body reactions when you experience the feeling of loneliness. What is happening to your heart rate? Do you experience cold sweats, sweaty palms, throat or chest constriction, or the sensation of falling? Specific techniques can help you to cope with the strong emotions and associated body reactions generated by stressful situations.

Chapter 4

Acculturation Stress and Chronic Stress

In the 1920s, the physiologist Walter Cannon introduced the concept of "stress" in medicine. Before this, the word "stress" was used mainly in physics to describe tensions against an object. In the 1930s, Hans Selye discovered that a surprising number of adverse conditions could provoke a particular set of symptoms in the animals in his research laboratory. He observed that under various conditions, which at first did not seem to have a lot in common (for example, injections or overcrowded cages), similar symptoms appeared: the animals lost weight and became more susceptible to infections, and their autopsy results showed a high proportion of stomach ulcers. Selye made the hypothesis that many and various tensions against an organism weaken its internal balance. Nowadays, we are familiar with the concept of stress, but at that time it was a daring hypothesis and Selye was considered a controversial researcher.

Selye described an adaptation syndrome nowadays called stress-response. Tensions start to produce an excessive amount of adrenal hormones, which in turn produce a number of unwelcome events in the adrenal system, brain, and body. Stress targets the immune system in particular, but at the time of Selye's studies little was known about the immune system, so the stress hypothesis remained a controversial topic for decades. The discovery of how the organs and fluids form the immune system is rather recent in the history of medicine, and the study of their relationships with the brain is even more recent (the term "psychoneuroimmunology" was coined in the seventies). There is, at present, a burst of activity in scientific circles as researchers try to unravel the relationships between psychological and physical stressors and their negative impact on immune functions and diseases, in particular on heart disease and depression.

Until it reaches the point where the immune system is weakened, stress is, in fact, an essential tool for survival. When tension lasts for a very short time – for a few minutes or a few days, for example – far from being harmful to your health, it enables you to react quickly and sharply, and it mobilizes the nervous system within seconds.

For example, say you moved to Australia and, after a wonderful afternoon diving in the Great Barrier Reef, you are driving home along a familiar road next to a sunny beach. You are very happy and relaxed and listening to some cool rock music. Life is good. Suddenly, a kangaroo jumps out of the bushes and into the path of your vehicle.

The stress response is immediate in body and brain, enabling you to hit the brakes and avoid a collision. You find your heart is suddenly beating like crazy and you are sweating and shaking. You just had one of those frights you will not soon forget; one second later on the brakes, and you could have lost control of your vehicle.

The cascade of reactions in your body, triggered by the nervous system responsible for accelerating energy use, happens extremely quickly: your heart rate accelerates; glucose is sent in high quantities via the blood to feed your muscles with energy; your muscles prepare for action, readying you to run if necessary; you start to sweat; and you can see and hear better. You experience an intense feeling of energy and readiness for action. This is the fight-or-flight response: fight the danger or fly away from it (or sometimes freeze to observe it). In any case, it enables you to do something quickly to save your life or avoid injury. This set of reactions is linked by a nervous system called, in medical anatomy, the sympathetic system.

On the contrary, during quiet periods, another part of the nervous system takes the lead in managing your organs. This system, the parasympathetic system, soothes things in your body. For example, a few minutes after avoiding the accident, you will be able to drive calmly again; the parasympathetic nervous system will have slowed down your heart rate, decreased heart contractions, and signalled that sugar can be stored in your liver again.

So what happened in your body? When the stressful event occurred, cortisol was sent through your blood in high concentration, and this acted on your hypothalamus (a sort of central station in the brain when it comes to stress), causing it to shut down the stress response. But the nervous and hormonal systems responsible for generating the stress response are also programmed to send the body the message to rest afterwards. This amazing circle of hormones enables a self-regulation of stress, raising cortisol levels during a stressful event, lowering them to enable rest, and raising them again when a new stressful event arises, and so forth.

When stress is intense and repetitive, there are continuous bursts of cortisol sent into the blood and, therefore, into the brain. The problem is that another of the cortisol functions is to shut down the immune response. Thus, if stress is chronic and repeated over time, the immune system becomes desensitized to cortisol. After weeks or months of an intense stress regimen, the body and mind may reach exhaustion. If you are chronically stressed, you become less able to defend yourself against a common cold or flu, and – more critically – you can develop serious long-term diseases (in particular, heart diseases). At the psychological level, chronic stress affects mental health: long-term intense stress can be followed by depression and burnout.

Burnout is a psychological and physiological reaction that occurs when the body and brain cannot adapt to demands properly anymore. The body is no longer able to respond to small stresses, and there are no cortisol bursts to enable it to react properly because cortisol levels are always very high. This is described as a flattened cortisol response, because on a graph the cortisol levels appear as a flat line instead of climbing when there is stress and diminishing afterwards. Burnout is often seen in people with demanding jobs (e.g. nurses and teachers).

Extreme stress is often seen in people suffering from post-traumatic stress syndrome, such as in the cases of holocaust survivors, war survivors, and people who have been raped or mugged. Chronically stressed people are found in many other situations. A work place can be stressful, as can working full-time while taking care of children or taking care of a parent with a serious disease such as Alzheimer's. The most common powerful stressors in many cultures (besides natural disasters, wars, or famines) are the loss of a spouse, a divorce, or the loss of a job.

Basically, chronic stress can target anybody who is experiencing changes or who has many difficult tasks to do either all at once or over a long period of time. In such situations, the brain produces high levels of stress hormones regularly and this starts to have a harmful effect on body, brain and mind.

Risks of Chronic Stress after Arrival

Moving is a major source of chronic stress. It may seem odd to compare the stress of moving to other traumas because, on the surface, there does not seem to be a lot of distress or emotional turmoil involved with moving. However, because of the constant demand to adapt over many months, a move – and especially a move to another country – can lead to burnout, physical and mental exhaustion, and diseases.

Overall, short-term stresses are quite positive for mental health: stressing ourselves with challenging goals makes life more interesting and motivates people to learn or do new things. Life without stress would not feel normal. The ups and downs of daily life make us appreciate the quiet times or happy moments. Besides, it seems that short-term stress does not impair the immune system. The components of the immune system do not fluctuate within seconds or minutes: it takes hours or days to build up chemical responses to injuries. This suggests that cortisol ups and downs are not an issue for the immune system. Actually, some results even suggest that short-term stress might boost the immune system, although there is debate about this among specialists. The problem is really about stress becoming chronic.

Chronic stress is generated by life circumstances but also by our own thoughts. We have seen in the previous chapter how to deal with the painful and automatic thoughts (stemming from anger, resent, regrets, worries, self-depreciation, or a sense of isolation and loneliness) that can become self-destructive and impair our relationships after a while.

Robert Sapolsky explains and illustrates vividly in his book *Why Zebras Don't Get Ulcers* that many of our stresses come from worries that are exacerbated by unhealthy lifestyles (lack of physical activity, overwork, and social isolation). We evolved to deal with very short-term stresses; our instinct is to run and hide from predators to avoid being the next dish on their menu. Evolutionarily, we are not prepared for stressors such as being stuck in a traffic jam on Monday mornings with a baby screaming in the back seat. However, we can help our body and diminish the negative impact of chronic stress. In the coming exercise, we will learn a technique that is at the core of stress-reduction programmes. In the first instance, we will learn to deal with the effects of stress on physical functions (breathing and heart rate). Then, once we start to master body relaxation, we will use visualisation to better deal with painful thoughts associated with body reactions.

Overwhelming Emotions

After arriving in a new country, many issues have to be solved, and this can take up a huge amount of time. Nevertheless, it is a good idea to take some extra time (but not necessarily too much) to develop some coping skills and to practise relaxation. Even though it feels very counterintuitive, relaxation in fact saves time because it enables us to calm down, organize our thoughts, and make better decisions based on what is really important.

In a plane, flight attendants tell passengers to put their own oxygen mask on first before helping others. That is what we are going to do now: oxygenate your body first, creating more space for positive thoughts in your mind. Then you will be more prepared and in better shape to go further. The following set of exercises will play the role of an oxygen mask, especially if you feel very anxious and worried at this moment in your life. They are designed to bring back the energy and strength you need to carry on with your new life and to continue to learn and to develop. After learning these techniques, you will be much stronger and better able to communicate, find your place in your new social circles, and eventually help and support others.

The Benefits of Deep Breathing on Stress Reduction

Breathe! Deep breathing exercises are very simple to understand and to practise and have been proven to reduce anxiety, depression, and irritability, as well as some physical symptoms caused or amplified by stress, such as pain, muscle tension, headaches, and fatigue. The main idea is to learn to use your lungs to their maximum potential by practising abdominal (or diaphragm) breathing. Breathing exercises are the key to relaxation because they help slow down many body functions. This should be first on your list of stress-reduction strategies.

It does not take very long to learn to switch from thoracic breathing to abdominal or deep breathing. It also does not take much time to practise this as a part of your daily routine. Here is a basic exercise.

Deep Breathing

For beginners, it is easier to learn deep breathing while lying down, but you can also try this in the sitting position.

— Make sure your position is comfortable. Put one hand on your abdomen and the other hand on your chest so you can feel the movements of both parts and become aware of your breathing patterns.

— First, breath normally through your nose and feel what happens. Which part of the body moves: your chest, abdomen, or both? Breathe without effort and feel the abdomen and your chest move as you inhale air.

— Next, when you inhale, create or increase the feeling of your abdomen expanding and rising by increasing abdominal breathing. To do this, imagine you are filling your abdomen with air, as if it were a balloon. Inhale slowly and fill first your abdomen, then the middle chest, and then the upper chest, all without raising your shoulders.

— Return to normal breathing and then try to breathe deeply again (try this for two minutes to start with, alternating deep breathing with normal breathing).

— If you are very tense, it might be difficult to achieve deep breathing, but this is when you need it the most; therefore, try it for just two minutes, and then try it again later during the day. Do this for several days in a row until it feels natural.

Deep breathing is something you should practise without forcing it. Relax your body, your shoulders and the muscles of your face. If it helps, you can close your eyes and imagine you are lying on the warm sand of a peaceful beach, being lulled by the sounds of the lapping waves....

Why is this useful? When you breathe deeply and slowly, the parasympathetic system takes over: your blood pressure goes down, your heart beats more slowly, the stress hormones are less active, and sugar gets stored instead of being sent to your muscles. This means there is less lactic acid build-up in your muscles and the levels of oxygen and carbon dioxide in the blood become balanced. In the long term, your immune system response is improved.

Body Relaxation and Visualisation

If you enjoyed the previous exercise then you will find it natural to go to the next stage and learn to relax your entire body. To do this, you must think about the muscular parts of your body and learn to consciously relax them, one after another, to ultimately reach a state where all (or most) muscles of the body are at rest. After a few minutes of a body relaxation session, it may feel like you are about to fall asleep… and many people actually do fall asleep. It might be wise to turn on an alarm clock if you have something to do afterwards.

Let's try a short exercise. This is something I learned to practise just after sports training when I was a teenager. The instructions are so simple that even after many years I can still remember them.

Relaxation

— Lying down comfortably, practise deep breathing (see previous exercise) for about two minutes.

— Now relax the muscles in every part of your body, starting with your feet and moving upwards progressively until you end with the face and tongue muscles. Relax each part of the body one by one as you focus on it.

— Start with your right foot: become aware of its tension and of your ability to move if you want it to, and then relax it. Pretend it is very heavy and that you cannot move it any longer. Take your time to feel this sensation.

— Once you feel it, move your focus up your leg and do the same to the muscles there. (You can also gently contract them for one second first, but this is not necessary). Feel how the tension goes away when you experience your leg muscles as heavy and unmoveable.

— Do the same for the other foot, lower parts of the leg, and upper parts. Continue upwards and relax the rest of the body the same way, taking your time and going progressively one area at a time: abdomen (stomach), right hand, right forearm, right upper arm, left hand, left forearm, left upper arm, upper chest and back, shoulders, neck, face and tongue.

— It takes some time, perhaps fifteen to twenty minutes, to do it all correctly. The time is worth it, however, as it feels so good afterwards! If you practise this several times, for instance once a day or a couple of times per week, you will soon be able to shorten this time and become very relaxed in only a few minutes.

Perhaps the reason I remember this exercise so well is because after our sports team practiced this we would have one minute of visualisation. While we were still totally relaxed, our coach would ask us to imagine being surrounded by the colour blue, and then to imagine this blue is the sky, and then that we are lying on the beach gazing up at the blue sky. It was incredibly relaxing after a hard training session. If you live in a cold part of the world like me, try this on a cold, dark, and rainy day; it will feel wonderful. With just your imagination, you can create your perfect place during a visualisation exercise: a wonderful garden full of colourful flowers, or green woods filled with the music of the leaves as they are caressed by the wind, or a warm vantage point over the Grand Canyon during sunset. Find your own place.

If you enjoy this exercise, you can go much further with your imagination: you can use your creativity to meet with an imaginary coach or to build something entirely new. You can actually experience a very active state of mind while your body is totally relaxed, and this provides you with the ability to focus much better than you can in ordinary life when surrounded by distractions. This is used in some meditation techniques, so if you are interested in relaxation and visualisation, you will probably very much enjoy learning meditation.

Making these practices a ritual helps. You could burn some special scents, listen to relaxing music, or choose a special place and moment in the week. Ritual helps because of our ability to learn automatically. This is called "classic conditioning" (as described by Pavlov who conducted the famous experiments in which dogs started to salivate when they heard a bell that usually indicated the arrival of food). You will quickly learn to associate your personal rituals (perfume, music, light, time of the day) to relaxing feelings. After practising them only a couple of times, relaxing becomes easier and the relaxed stage is reached more rapidly.

Emotion Control Using the Focus Technique

The next exercise is based on relaxation techniques. This exercise diminishes unpleasant and painful emotions (such as loneliness) and is particularly useful when you feel you may be overreacting to a situation or when you are feeling anxious.

The focus technique is a form of visualisation done during relaxation (you can find similar approaches in mindfulness and in some other meditation techniques). The objective is to develop a better ability to regulate anxiety, fear, and body reactions (such as stress and tension) and to learn how to experience certain thoughts without automatically experiencing the unwanted bodily reactions (such as an increased heart rate, cold sweats, feelings of oppression in the throat and chest, and other reactions). The key is to train yourself to think about the situations or ideas that usually generate anxious feelings while you are experiencing a relaxed state with your body. When you train yourself to associate these thoughts with a relaxed state, you enable yourself to experience the thoughts without (or with only very mild versions of) the body reactions.

This does take some courage. This visualisation exercise can be difficult, emotionally speaking, because you must evoke and experience strong negative emotions again. Using the ABCDE technique described earlier, you can think about issues from a certain distance, whereas in the focus exercise you will re-experience the body reactions directly, which will be very disagreeable in the first instance. To succeed, you must proceed with little steps. The rewards are great: if you manage to complete the exercise a few times, it should help you tremendously in the future.

The focus technique was developed by Western therapists. I will provide basic instructions for trying it on your own, but some people find it difficult to relax and visualise and may need extra help, a coach, or a therapist. Try this exercise to smother emotions that are very disagreeable. It is useful not only when you feel you are overreacting to a situation but also when a situation does not make sense.

Let's have a look at a real situation in which relaxation and visualisation helped to solve an issue. Siegel, the clinical psychologist mentioned earlier who uses mindfulness and relaxation techniques to treat his patients, reports a personal example in one of his books: When his firstborn cried, he experienced anxiety to an extent he knew was not normal. It happened several times, so he began to reflect on it, trying to understand where his anxiety came from. He wondered if perhaps it came from the way he had been raised by his own parents, but no specific memory came back to him.

One day, when the baby was crying and he was experiencing this emotion again, he decided to close his eyes and let himself evoke whatever images and memories came back to him. The images and sounds that came back to him were from an experience he had as a young intern, as a doctor for young children: at the time, he had no choice but to hear a lot of children screaming as he drew blood from them, which had been extremely painful for him since he had to carry on with the medical procedures in spite of the children's pain. He realized that when his own baby cried, he was experiencing the same emotional reactions he had had back then, and this is where the massive anxiety was coming from.

This awareness enabled him to better cope with this emotion because now he had identified it and its source, and he knew how to use visualisation to calm his anxiety over this situation (this is what we will learn in the coming exercise). He also talked about it with people who had similar experiences, and this helped him a lot too. This is also something to keep in mind when having issues: sharing with others who are going through the same issues helps tremendously. We will go further into this later.

To use the focus technique, first spend a few minutes experiencing deep breathing and body relaxation in a lying or in a sitting position. Then, evoke images and thoughts of a painful situation and learn to listen to your body while doing so, increasing your body awareness and trying to understand the roots of your feelings (for example, when thinking about loneliness).

Read the instructions for the next exercise and then find a quiet moment to begin your practise.

Focus Your Mind

This exercise was inspired by the work of Ann Weiser Cornell, *The Power of Focusing*, 1996.

— Start with a short relaxation technique in a sitting or lying position. It is not necessary to close your eyes. You can use a pen and paper to write down your impressions and ideas.

— Focus on one thing that has been a problem for you: an emotion, a person, or a situation.

— As you focus on this idea, become aware of how it feels in your body. Notice the sensations in your throat, tensions in your muscles, pains in some parts of your body. Let them express themselves, and let them be. Become very aware of them without fear and without judging yourself. This part of the exercise can be difficult, so continue to breathe regularly and relax your muscles.

— As you feel physical reactions, tensions, and pains, acknowledge their presence. To help you, you can talk mentally to yourself by welcoming these body sensations. , the therapist who published this technique, advises people to "say hello" to their feelings as a way to acknowledge them. By acknowledging a negative feeling and its physical sensations, you decrease its power over you.

— As you acknowledge and accept these sensations, they will become progressively less painful, less invasive. This is because you are in a relaxed state, breathing regularly, and training your brain to associate these difficult thoughts to a new physiological state. You are conditioning yourself to experience peace and relaxation when these feelings arrive.

— You can write down your experience if you wish.

— Train yourself a few times over on the same issues to continue the work of diminishing their impact on your body reactions. Become able to experience these thoughts without judging yourself; instead, continue to "say hello" to the emotions and physical reactions that the thoughts evoke.

If you feel extremely sad, to the extent that you are thinking that life is not worth it and you are thinking about death, or if you are crying on a daily basis or experiencing symptoms of pain, lack of sleep, or a strong anxiety that prevents you from going out of your house to meet the real world, then cognitive exercises or relaxation exercises done at home will not be enough; you must consult a medical doctor (always check your health first before assuming symptoms are due to stress) and ask for assistance in finding a good mental health professional to help you.

The focus technique involves recreating the painful feelings in a safe environment. Evoking these feelings may bring tears and feel just as painful as the real situation did, and this is exactly why it is important to have this experience in a quiet and safe place. As you mentally evoke the situations and thoughts associated with disagreeable feelings, unwanted body reactions and sensations take place (tears, accelerated heartbeat, sweaty palms, or a feeling a tightness in the throat). Old memories can also surface, aggravating these body reactions.

The most important thing is to reassure yourself that you are safe. Do not be judgmental or harsh with yourself when you recall these feelings. On the contrary, remind yourself that these feelings are part of being a human; these are very universal feelings that alert us to undesirable situations so we can act towards taking better care of ourselves.

The focus technique works because it enables you to associate a very disagreeable feeling with new, more agreeable sensations. The same principles are used in cognitive therapies to help people rid themselves of some of their fears: the disagreeable stimuli (an image or situation) is present, but you experience it in a safe environment and, as you experience it again and again and reassure yourself that it is safe, you become progressively more comfortable with it. The pain and distress associated with the thoughts will diminish. Feelings will not necessarily go away completely, but they will not be so overwhelming and painful anymore.

If you find this exercise difficult to do, perhaps it is because you are still judging yourself and thinking your feelings are not normal. If so, ask yourself why you think this way. Try to analyse your reactions with the ABCDE technique presented earlier. This might help you to figure out that your reactions could be less intense.

Using the Focus Technique in Daily Life

After practising the focus technique a few times, you will be prepared to recognize immediately the warning signals of anxiety and other painful feelings in your daily life. You can then take action instead of letting yourself react with your usual automatic behaviours, for example, crying or going out and getting drunk.

You now have a better mastery of your emotional reactions and can try to react differently. If you realize the painful clinching of the throat is just a symptom of loneliness, you can choose to call some friends or go out and find some company, or you can go to a healing place where you feel good. Instead of being overwhelmed by the feelings, a choice has become possible: you can calm yourself, and the pain loses its intensity. This choice enables you to carry on with your life and, having heard the signals from your body and mind, to do something for yourself that will help you find a good internal balance. When difficult moments come, you will be better prepared to face difficult emotions because you have developed a better awareness about your own reactions and have worked on them.

That said, relaxation and visualisation are not a universal cure for every mental pain. Sometimes when you practise relaxation (and especially if you try it alone or if you are depressed), you end up thinking more about your issues than is necessary and, subsequently, feel even more down. Pay attention to how the techniques make you feel. Your coping methods must fit in with your personality and preferences.

Some people told me that they tried relaxation and hated it because it made them feel "too relaxed" and they associated it with being down or they feared they would become too slow in getting things done afterwards. Perhaps it doesn't work for some people, or perhaps they did not try hard enough, or perhaps there are moments in life when we are simply not ready for it. There may be obstacles that prevent us from practising relaxation and visualisation. If you experience sadness and frustration after trying relaxation and visualisation (or the focus technique) on your own, and if you still think it leads nowhere after trying several times, do not force yourself to continue. Instead, if you have emotions that are very difficult to deal with, you could seek professional help from a relaxation advisor, a meditation coach, or a psychotherapist. You could also try the ABCDE technique or simply come back to the focus technique later when you feel ready.

Physical Activity as a Stress Buffer

A very important feature of most stress-management programmes is physical activity. Regular physical activity benefits almost every aspect of your mind and body: it strengthens bones, muscles, and joints; it has a positive impact on lungs and cardiovascular functions; it boosts immune functions; and it slows down some of the natural ageing processes in our body and brain. It also has immediate benefits: it helps us to eliminate toxins and digest food, to sleep better and combat insomnia, and to feel less tired and more energetic. Recent research suggests exercise can help reduce anxiety and stress, lift the mood, and help people become more resilient.

There are other benefits to exercising for internationals: it is a fun way to meet new people, especially if you join a sports team. This is a more efficient way to meet new people than, for example, by attending parties, because the sport makes it easy to find an initial topic of conversation: you automatically have at least one interest in common. Being part of a team also ensures that you will meet the same people regularly, and it makes it more likely that you will socialize and perhaps build long-lasting friendships. Also, in most sports clubs, new members join often, so your circle of friends can be extended progressively.

If you found it hard to go to the gym or to go for a run several times a week in your home country, it might be even more difficult in the new place. Read what these expats experienced and shared with humour:

> — I attended a yoga class, but I did not understand the language precisely enough. Not easy when, after standing on your head, you cannot understand how to get back on your feet. I remained standing on my head longer than I really wanted to! (laugh)
> *Gail, UK*
> *2 years abroad (the Netherlands)*

> — I tried the aqua gym only once: it was just after my arrival. I could not understand much of the language then, and I could not see the movements that the others were doing because, of course, it was all under water ... at least I learned to count to eight!
> *Corine, France*
> *5 years abroad (Belgium, Germany, the Netherlands)*

Personally, it took me a while to join a sports team because I was embarrassed that I did not speak the language well enough. However, the obstacles were only in my head; as soon as I joined a team, I learned the basic vocabulary of the sport in Dutch, and that was enough information to have fun with others – with the bonus that I was also able to practise my language skills. At first, I felt odd and uncomfortable, but after a few weeks it rapidly became a familiar place where it felt good to go and meet people. It became an "Ibasho" (the explanation for this word is next page; stay tuned). I started to spend time with my teammates outside of training hours, and over time we became good friends. Whenever I felt alone or tired, the sports club was the place that gave me some energy back.

In terms of stress management, a sports club is a holistic solution: friends, fun, sports, a familiar environment... all in one place. It might take courage to start and to keep going, but it is really worth it.

Chapter 5

Home Abroad

The Japanese language offers a word that has no equivalent in English or in Latin languages: Ibasho. Ibasho describes a place we associate with feelings of home, comfort, and safety: a place we are used to going.

Being in a new place and being surrounded by strangers generates lots of anxiety. Remember your first day of school: the new smell of the big classroom, your heart beating strongly, and the tightness in your throat? As an adult, we may have less extreme symptoms but we still experience higher levels of anxiety in new places than we do in familiar places.

In animals studied in a laboratory, it has been shown that when the animal is moved to a new place, the brain activates the same centres in the sub-cortex that are activated by fear. Just like other mammals, we need time before a sense of familiarity builds up and before the initial anxiety gives way to a sense of peace.

Feeling Good in a New Place

To lower our stress level, it is important to find a place that feels like home: a familiar place in which we know where things are and how things work, and where we can quietly read a book or enjoy a nice conversation with a friend without wishing we were somewhere else.

You may remember a place where you used to go regularly and where you felt at home. Perhaps it was a café at the street corner where you enjoyed going in the morning or a pub where you went with colleagues after work. It feels like home wherever we meet regularly with the same people, even if we only vaguely know them and they are not true friends (for example, neighbours we meet at the bakery). Regular contact with familiar people makes us feel safe. Whether you are in Africa or Asia, it helps to find a place you feel you are welcome to go any time to just sit there and chat.

Familiar settings can help even when they lack the opportunity for human contact. Personally, I have found several such places. My favourite is a little wood near my apartment. The sound of the trees and birds remind me of some very old memories of my childhood. We used to live a few kilometres down the road from a large forest, and, from time to time (but not often), my father drove us there. It was always a big event and a treat. We would spend an afternoon searching for mushrooms or lily flowers in the woods with my parents and siblings. Now, when I go running or walking in the woods nearby, I always walk more slowly, listen to birds, and stop at some point to enjoy the place, admire some big tree, or listen to the wind. Before I return to my busy life, I spend a few moments there feeling good and finding my roots again. This is what is meant by Ibasho.

There is no rule, it seems, to where you will find Ibasho. The huge variety of human experience drives internationals to enjoy Ibasho in a variety of places, and one individual's reactions to a place are often totally the opposite of the next person's.

> — *My Ibasho must be contrary, somewhere in the noisy crowd. Just a day ago, I talked to a man from Kolkata [India]: his worst experience was among the fields in the middle of nowhere, when, from the farmhouse to the nearest supermarket, there was a distance of about 7 km! He was about running outside to scream at the clouds: AAAAAA!*
> Tatiana (anonymous comment on my blog)

Tatiana's example is such a good example of our diversity. Have you found your Ibasho? Japanese gardens have been built to generate a relaxing feeling. Is there one near your place? Is there a park nearby where you can recreate this feeling? Or are you more like Tatiana and love crowded cities and busy open-air markets?

When finding or recreating your Ibasho, think about all your senses. In nature, this can be the sound of the waves or birds or the wind in the tree leaves. Amongst human civilization, you will probably be attracted by certain background music. In your new apartment or house, you can carry with you the smells, foods, and melodies from your past life, and from these memories you will recreate your home.

Old Memories

Our brains do not have a dedicated place to store memories, because this would soon be overwhelmed with information. For instance, a holiday is not remembered like a movie, sequence after sequence; and a piece of music is not remembered in its entirety with all its musical instruments playing, as it would be on a CD or memory stick. Instead, our brain extracts information from several areas and links them together to form overall impressions.

For example, if you remember a holiday at the beach on a sunny day, the blue colour is stored in the visual part of your brain (in the extreme lower back of the brain called the occipital lobe), while the sounds of the waves are stored in auditory areas (in the temporal lobes, near your ears), and the associated memories of specifics such as trees, white buildings, gulls flying in the sky, and other details are stored in other parts of the brain. The sounds you think you remember from this particular moment – for example, the sounds of crashing waves – are not necessarily the sounds you heard on that particular day. Instead, it is more likely that you are recalling the sounds of waves you have heard and stored over various times in your life. Few of our memories are specific; they tend to be vague and distorted. This is why we love our holiday pictures and carry back souvenirs or tokens of remembrance; these items would not be so precious if our memories were more reliable.

A token or a detail in our environment can suddenly evoke more specific memories that we had partially or entirely forgotten: the fragrance of a former lover, the music we were dancing to when we were still in middle school, and the taste of a dish that our grandfather cooked for us on New Year's Eve may bring back details we thought we had forgotten. We then have the impression that these specific memories were there all along. The same networks in our brain that were activated at those times are activated all over again, and we feel as though we have travelled back in time. This can be an enjoyable experience: dozens of good memories of the people and situations that gave us feelings of happiness can come flooding back to us.

It is important to enjoy some of these memories and sensations from time to time. It feels good to be "back home" in our minds. This is why it might be important for you to pack your old CDs, furniture, photo albums, or familiar foods in with your luggage.

Smells and foods are particularly powerful at evoking past memories and emotions, and, after visiting their family during holiday season, many internationals carry back foods and fragrances they miss. When a specific festivity is approaching (Christmas, for example), we internationals miss not only our family and friends but also the associated smells of the good foods or specific flowers, the cold or warm weather of home, and the traditions such as Christmas trees. These can become a beautiful nostalgic memory or a painful reminder of what we miss, depending on our state of mind.

Experiencing these past melodies, smells, or foods in your new situation can reactivate old memories that would be almost impossible to consciously activate. The small things that evoke good old times can bring back a feeling of being at home and help to build a bridge between good old memories and the good new memories you are forming, effectively reconciling your past with the present. If you are someone who is prone to homesickness, merging old memories with new experiences can help.

Here are some sound pieces of advice that internationals gave when I asked what they would advise a good friend to do to feel at home when living abroad:

> — When I became able to communicate (in English), it changed many things. Also the fact that we didn't leave anything in France. We took everything with us: furniture, books, etc., and so our house here was home. And it's stupid but also the fact that we know all the things that make up our everyday life: what day is the trash truck passing, what is where, etc. My best advice would be don't run away from [your new] home when you have holidays; spend your holidays in your foster country, otherwise your children will never feel at home. Visit the country, and don't criticise the habits that are different from yours.
> Christine, French,
twelve years abroad (the Netherlands)

> — I haven't found a place to feel at home. I've gotten used to not feeling at home and take pleasure in my son and husband being at home here. They did it by joining sports clubs.
> Sarah, US citizen,
four years abroad (Ireland, the Netherlands)

> — Allow yourself some pleasures that help you feel at home/at ease; find a place to live that you like and do not avoid; pay for a small shipment of belongings that are dear to you; buy the nice ingredients at the store if you feel like it, even if they are more expensive than you are used to; go for dinner in a nice place; do not feel bad for hanging out with other expats instead of nationals of the country you moved to (it might be easier to relate to expats at first, and that helps ease in the transition).
> Ike, lived thirteen years abroad as a child
(Sweden, Ghana, the Netherlands, France, Mexico)
and six as an adult (Cambodia, Thailand, Congo, Senegal)

Should You Stay or Should You Go?

Is it a good idea to return home when you cannot cope with living abroad because you feel homesick? There is no simple answer to this question.

You may be experiencing lots of sadness and anxiety or perhaps having issues in your marriage or struggling with addiction, drinking, or eating disorders. You may feel intense loneliness and have the sense of being stuck in life, and the pain you are experiencing could make you think you should leave. However, try to be aware that many life issues are rooted in our way of dealing with obstacles and are not necessarily the obstacles themselves.

We have patterns and automatic ways of reacting to life circumstances, of interacting with people, and sometimes of judging (ourselves and others). These patterns are very strong and do not change easily. Most are due to our personality and early life circumstances. They can change during life only when we can do something to change and grow, and when we decide to develop new ways of thinking. They rarely depend on external circumstances.

If you feel miserable living abroad, and this has been going on for many months or years, it is not transition stress anymore; it is chronic stress, and we've seen in a previous chapter how this damages your health. But will leaving the country solve your issues, or will this just be a distraction until you settle down again and face the same types of issues again?

Leaving for another place may help and may bring some feelings of relief in the short-term, but very soon the same issues will return because they have the same roots; you carry your issues with you. By issues, I mean patterns of thoughts and behaviours and ways of interpreting and reacting to reality, many of which can lead to problems and suffering for yourself or for the people close to you.

External circumstances, such as your move abroad and the new place, can exacerbate these painful feelings. However, if you learn to overcome your issues under difficult circumstances instead of running away from the situation or environment, you will gain more freedom and strength afterwards. If you flee from situations without facing these issues, you will most likely encounter similar issues in another place and time, and you will not have learned how to deal with them. You will once again suffer and feel that life has been unfair to you, because the same things will happen again. However, the common factor is you: you must learn to overcome some difficulties, wherever you are. The sooner you can do this, the less painful life will be.

If you have a family – a partner or perhaps children – and you want to leave, ask yourself what the consequences will be for the other family members. When the family has to go back "home" because one person has not adapted to the new situation, there may be more issues when you arrive back than there were before your departure. Are you ready to deal with this? This is a question you should address before considering departure. What might the consequences be for each family member, and how will you help them deal with these?

On the other hand, there are also situations where you should definitely leave. For example, you should leave if your security is compromised by an unstable political situation that puts the security of foreigners at risk; if your spouse has become psychologically or physically abusive (a situation that happens too often when one person becomes vulnerable through being isolated and financially dependent); or if your parents or grown-up children need you back home. When security or health is at stake, returning home for your own safety or to support your family is probably the best option.

However, if the reason you want to go back home relates to your personal difficulties in adapting to a new place, it is a good idea to think further and to try to overcome this obstacle before making a final decision.

> *— Home is where I live. I've been depressed in different countries, and it had nothing to do with the countries themselves. Being an expat does not make you depressed or unhappy; it is just how you deal with it.*
> Gabrielle, French,
> thirteen years abroad (Switzerland, Russia, England, the Netherlands, Scotland)

At some point during her expat life, leaving the country was very tempting for Gabrielle (in the testimony above), but she realized that the country was not the only problem. Gabrielle first followed a course of therapy where she learned to be less of a perfectionist and also to listen to and respect her own needs. The entire family benefited from this, and in her next two moves abroad she was able to manage the transition much better. In particular, she rapidly built a community of friends and organized many weekend outings for the family to relax and have fun. When she did leave a country, it was for professional reasons and not in an attempt to change her feelings of sadness and exhaustion.

Assess your situation carefully. If you can find the strength to deal with the issues you are facing instead of fleeing from them, you will end up a much stronger person and have much more freedom for the rest of your life.

Manage Painful Feelings

Neurologically, different systems in different areas of the brain process negative and positive feelings. The system that processes disagreeable emotions and pain reacts to punishment and drives us to avoid some situations. The other system processes the pleasurable feelings, the wants and the likes. They are both complex reward systems and learning systems and are relatively autonomous, which implies that our progress towards well-being involves at least two roads: one that diminishes disagreeable and painful feelings and one that augments our exposure to agreeable moments in our daily life.

Painful or destructive thoughts and feelings cannot be avoided. We will never live in a world without pain: mental pain is part of life. However, there are at least two things we can do to alleviate painful and destructive thoughts. We can accept them by acknowledging their presence when they arrive, and, to put it simply, we can learn to avoid feeling bad about feeling bad. This is achieved by augmenting self-compassion and diminishing inner self-criticism. We can also learn how to prevent or stop harmful thoughts from invading our mental life. They will come to us from time to time, but they should not be in the background of our mind all day long.

We cannot, however, simply suppress all painful feelings and associated thoughts, probably because they support vital functions. Humans have evolved over millions of years, and the neurological functions we have built up are what enabled our species to survive. Disagreeable feelings are there for important reasons: Unhappiness and feelings of discontent, even depression, can motivate people to change, thereby boosting creativity and adaptation (psychological resilience develops when we face difficult situations or adversity, and our confidence builds up when we prove to ourselves that we are able to handle these difficult situations). Pessimism can be a good thing: it enables us to maintain low expectations and thereby avoid disappointments and feelings of helplessness, and in risky situations it helps us to act carefully. Loneliness is a signal that we need to seek the company of others.

Therapists and researchers who work on helping people to build coping skills in various areas of their life come to the same conclusion: to be able to thrive amidst life's adversities, it is important to develop techniques that enable us to honour and use our emotions. It is useless to try to avoid our emotions or to feel guilty about the way we feel. For example, what is the point of feeling guilty or bad about yourself for feeling lonely? The feeling of loneliness has a place and a role to play in your mental life, and the first step to making it less invasive is to acknowledge it.

I am not saying that we should enjoy painful and negative emotions but that we should accept their existence and acknowledge their message. We have to learn to listen to ourselves and to our body reactions and then, instead of reacting with self-criticism, react as we would for a good friend: listen and show compassion. Self-compassion helps us to become more aware of painful feelings and reactions, and, as a consequence, these things lose their powerful impact.

Sharing negative emotions such as fear, anger, despair, and sadness also has positive functions: when we share our negative thoughts with another person in a conversation – for example, when we share our questions or confusion over an issue – we feel understood. Listening to a person and sharing issues creates strong bonds between two people; it builds trust and intimacy. This is particularly strong between parents and children, friends, or love partners.

John Gottman, a specialist in relationship issues, and Siegel, a specialist in early traumas, have proposed programmes aimed at helping individuals, parents, and couples to increase their awareness of negative emotions, acknowledge these feelings in themselves and in the person they love, avoid letting the feelings get under their skin, and learn to express them in a way that strengthens their bonds with others.

Add Positive Experiences

Psychologists have shown that we should increase the frequency, diversity, and quality of our positive feelings. The idea that we can cultivate positivity is relatively new in science, even though it is quite easy to understand intuitively.

Seligman, a psychologist who has made psychological resilience and learned helplessness his speciality, officially created the field of positive psychology at a conference in 1999. He was not the first to develop such ideas, but from the moment he defined the new field and gave it its name an official society with its own publications was born, and this field of research is still rapidly expanding.

Frederickson, a leading scientist in this field, proposed a model to predict the optimal amount of positivity needed to blossom in life. She defined positive experiences as joy, gratitude, serenity, interest, hope, pride, amusement, inspiration, awe, and love. The statistician working with her on this project, Marcial Losada, had previously developed models that predicted the success and creativity of teams working in a business environment.

In 2005, Frederickson and Losada concluded that people who experience three positive experiences against one negative experience on average (for example, within a week) have a high level of emotional well-being and a better ability to bounce back from life events. These people are energized by positivity, tend to be more creative than those with lower positive-experience ratios, and are ready to learn and grow further in their life. Nowadays, positive psychology researchers such as Frederickson, Seligman, Sonia Lyubomirsky, Alex Linley, and many others suggest that it is advisable to work actively at increasing the quality and amount of positive experiences in our daily lives.

Positive experiences depend on personality and preferences and, therefore, take many varied forms, such as expressing gratitude, cultivating good relationships, helping others, exercising and maintaining good health and good eating habits, committing to a meaningful goal, practising religion and spirituality, enjoying and enhancing the small pleasures of life, and increasing flow experiences, etc. The possibilities are infinite, but our access to them depends on our state of mind, which is not fully but certainly to a large extent under our control.

Positivity gives us more freedom to think and to act. Positive emotions seem to have the potential to broaden people's ideas about possible actions: joy sparks the urge to plan and to be creative, and interest sparks the urge to explore and to learn; on the contrary, negative emotions make our behaviours far less creative and easier to predict.

To summarize, one of the lessons from recent psychology and neuroscience research is that to build resilience, promote happiness, and increase our long-term well-being, we should do our best to diminish the pain coming from disagreeable emotions and harmful thoughts (on a daily or weekly basis) while simultaneously working to add positivity (joy, serenity, love, etc.) into our lives. This process is associated with finding fulfilment in life.

Here is my personal definition of happiness: finding a meaning in life not by thinking too much about it but by simply finding our place in the society and discovering the tasks we are appreciated for and enjoy doing. This is something that takes a lot of time to build in a new environment, and it cannot be done immediately after arrival when there are so many urgent things to organize and settle. However, after a while (after a few months or a couple of years in the new country), it is worth thinking about what living abroad brings you in the long-term. Look back and observe the strengths you gained and the new horizons this opened for you – think again about your main objectives in life.

Living in a new environment challenges your identity, and this is scary, but it also gives you the opportunity to raise your personal ambitions, start new projects, find fulfilment, and redefine what makes you who you are.

PART 2

SOCIAL LIFE

Chapter 6

Cultural Differences in Values and Attitudes

Earlier, when I introduced you to exercises that would help you deal with the stress issues generated by arriving in a new country, I implicitly used a disease model, assuming that the entire experience of moving and living abroad could put your health at risk during the first months. This type of approach focuses on "pathologies" or risks but not on the strengths gained from the experience. For a long time, the pathological model has been the most common approach in the field of health and psychology: historically, psychologists' and mental health professionals' main objective was to treat or lower the suffering of patients.

However, some researchers specialising in immigration started to challenge the pathological approach in the 1980s. They were interested in the positive side of the migration phenomenon and saw migrants as actors in a process of change and adaptation rather than as victims of a difficult condition.

Cross-cultural adaptation started to be studied systematically, – in particular, the processes of change that individuals and groups were experiencing on both sides (the immigrant and the host culture) and the interactions between the two.

This led to the development of cross-cultural learning programmes. The paradigm of the needy and weak migrant with increased health risks was replaced, or completed, by the idea that science should also provide tools to enable to understand and learn about cross-cultural adaptation and the benefits of cultural encounters on individuals and communities. Training programmes were developed to help individuals feel at ease in cross-cultural communication situations and get the most out of them. We will now use this approach, which I do not see as antagonistic but rather as complementary to the pathological model. We will also address the issues linked with cultural adaptation and social life abroad.

In this chapter, we examine some fundamental elements of cross-cultural knowledge. When you develop cross-cultural knowledge, you progressively open your mind to new ways of seeing and thinking: you can learn how locals think about situations and learn to understand their point of view. You do not necessarily agree with their point of view, but you learn to be aware of it in order to understand what has happened, what is happening, and what is likely to happen in the new environment.

While doing so, you will become aware of how your own culture has influenced your ways of perceiving, reacting, and thinking, and also of how the way you were raised has modelled your value system. Developing such insights is very valuable; it enables you to avoid reacting automatically to situations in the "old way." You may surprise yourself by thinking, "Hey, this way to react is so typical in the region I come from!" as if looking at your culture from a distance. You will then experience more or less of culture shock when back in your own culture (and this is one of the many reasons why repatriation is not necessarily easy).

To develop cultural awareness, it is important to reflect on your own way of thinking as compared to that of people in the host country. Therefore, the exercises in the present chapter take the form of questions that encourage self-reflection and cross-cultural comparisons. To raise your own awareness, take the time to pause and truly think about your own examples and your own ways of thinking. In doing so, you will benefit far more from this chapter than if you read it through without pausing.

Once you have a better understanding of the different ways of thinking and potentially reacting to similar situations, you can choose for yourself how you want to react: will you continue to react as you would have done in your own culture, or will you adapt your behaviours to fit in better with the locals' implicit expectations? It is your choice.

Knowledge of the choice gives you more freedom than if you only know how to react in an automatic way, as if you were still living in your own culture. Freedom comes from developing insights into the reasons for your reactions and, as a consequence, being able to choose between two or more alternatives rather than just falling into the automatic reactions you learned in your culture.

Roots of Cultural Differences

Some cultural differences are obvious and will entertain tourists: the interesting architecture, the different ways of dressing up, the bizarre foods or unusual traffic signs. It takes more effort and observation skills to become aware of the less superficial features of the culture and, in particular, of the way people regulate their behaviour, the rules of courtesy, the gestures or silences in conversations, the way they praise or criticise others, or the distance between people during interactions. And it becomes even more difficult to capture and understand the deeper-level differences, such as the values, beliefs, and attitudes that drive behaviours.

Most values and ways of behaving have been built over centuries or thousands years of civilisation. They are influenced by geography and natural forces, by dominant religions, by intellectuals (from Socrates to Confucius), by technologies and discoveries, and also by wars and their sequels. They evolve and change relatively slowly.

I have seen many expats failing in their adaptation because they had expected that locals would be different. For example, they may have expected the locals to be more efficient, and so they end up trying to influence those closest to them, hoping they will change to better fit their expectations. These expats tend to become progressively more sensitive and angry about the features of their host culture. They are so sure that their own values and their own ways of getting things done are the best or most important that they do not reflect on their own cultural biases. They hope that the locals will understand that there are more efficient ways of getting things done and will learn to adapt. And of course, it does not work, so the expats end up banging their heads against the wall.

Do not fight the system, even if you do not like it; the best you can do is to learn to deal with it and get what you need out of it. You will not change a system of thoughts moulded by centuries of culture. Besides, when you try to change someone else's behaviour, you are implicitly saying that there is something wrong with their culture. Are you sure you have really understood this culture in the first place?

You are the one who decided to travel, so you are the one who needs to adapt, and accepting this will force you to put your own thoughts in perspective. If you decide to stay and make the most out of your experience, you will have to become more flexible and tolerant. This is where understanding the other culture becomes critical.

Cultural Differences in Perceiving the World

We perceive and interpret the world based on what is already in our brains: everything is filtered through our previous experience, the knowledge we have developed since birth, and our interactions with our parents, other people, and the world surrounding us.

In a historic experiment, Alfred Yarbus provided a powerful illustration of how instructions given to a person before they are shown a picture influences the person's eye movements. The researcher used an eye-tracking technique to monitor where the participants focused their attention on a picture after they were given specific instructions. The results are presented in Figure 6.1. One participant's eye movements (represented by a continuous line) are shown in the series of graphs. Each graph represents a different condition based on a specific instruction given before the participant viewed the picture.

It is striking in the way that each result differs as a function of the instructions. When asked to evaluate the age of the character, the participant did not pay attention to the same details as when he received no instruction or when he was asked to evaluate whether or not the family is wealthy. His eye movements were influenced by his priming. Depending on what the participant considered important, his attention was diverted towards different areas of the same scene. In some cases, the background was most important; in other cases, the faces or the distance between the characters was most important.

The features the participants paid attention to were then stored (or not) in the memory; the focus of their attention strongly influenced the way they recollected a scene.

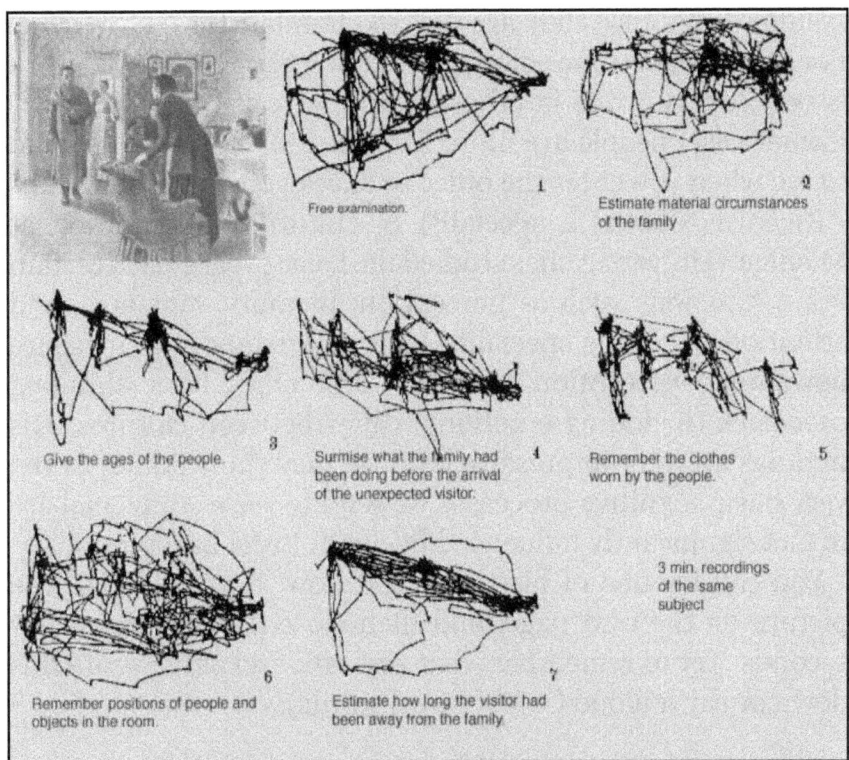

Picture 6.1. Results from Yarbus showing that the way a participant views a painting (upper left) depends on the instructions (see below each image) given before viewing (in Yarbus, A., *Eye Movements and Vision*, 1967).

This experiment illustrates how our perception is influenced by our intentions, expectations, or knowledge. It is not a passive process. We are not like sponges absorbing water. We direct our attention to the stimuli offered by the environment, and we can have a lot of control over it. If we do not pay attention to something, it is not seen, not processed, and of course not remembered either.

In the same way, we see (or hear, smell, or touch) the world through the lenses of our culture. The values transmitted by our culture make some things seem essential, and we neglect others because they do not seem important in our reference system or because they are just too familiar for us to notice. For example, in some countries, the way people dress for work is very formal while in others it can be very informal. In the former case, people are more likely to look at you from head to toe when you enter the office to check your presentation.

Richard Nisbett, a specialist of culture and cognition at Michigan University, has studied the basic processes of certain brain functions such as perception, memory, language, and attention. Nisbett's speciality is to understand and measure how much perception, memory, and other basic thinking processes (including emotions) differ between cultures. His findings are very impressive because they show that even the very basic cognitive processes we tend to see as universal are in fact significantly influenced by our cultural backgrounds.

You can try one of his tests right now: have a look at the picture on the next page, and then close the book for a few seconds. Try to remember what you saw, and either write this down or say it aloud (in your own words).

What did you recall? What did you recall first? There are large differences in the results for this type of task when Asians are compared to Westerners. Asians tend to describe a scene like this by describing the whole situation ("It looked like a seascape with..."), whereas the first sentence from Americans is three times more likely to refer to the fish in the foreground ("There were four big fish, two of them moving to the left...").

Similarly, Asians remember the background details better in a memory task, whereas Westerners tend not to pay much attention to the background and therefore do not remember it as well.

As humans, we all have a similar eye anatomy due to our common origins; i.e. we have the same vision cells that enable us all to see the same colours, shapes, and movements. What differs between us is the way we move our eyes to search for information; this aspect of our vision is determined by our brains. When you present participants of Asian and Western cultures with similar visual image, their average behaviour patterns will differ according to their culture. Asians tend to see the world as holistic: they look at the whole picture first and at the relationships between the elements. Westerners, on the other hand, tend to pay attention to the individual and most salient objects first rather than to the whole picture.

This phenomenon is very strong and has been replicated in various experiments with other types of images and cultures. Recently, brain imaging has corroborated the results by showing that the brain's process for solving abstract-picture problems differs between Americans and Asians.

According to Nisbett, these cultural differences can be observed in children from as early as two years old. Cultural differences in perception are rooted in perhaps hundreds or thousands of years of civilization, influencing children's early cognitive development and perpetuating ways of thinking from one generation to another via the early interactions of children and their cultural environment (for example, the way an adult interacting with a child will point and name objects and people in a scene).

Cultural differences are even more pronounced in the way social relationships are understood, in our beliefs regarding how we can influence the world around us, in our value systems, and in the many other thoughts and feelings we experience as we encounter various situations in our daily life. This is what we will explore now.

Cultural Diversity in Social Life

Researchers in the scientific fields of social psychology and organisational behaviour have observed fundamental differences in social interactions between cultures. Unlike Yarbus or Nisbett, social scientists rarely study participants who are solving computerized problems in artificial laboratory situations; they prefer to interview or observe people in their natural environment and to collect information on their attitudes, values, expectations, and behaviours in real-life situations. Based on answers from huge numbers of participants from various countries, they can then use explorative statistical techniques to discover what factors most influence certain behaviours in given situations.

In the '80s, Geert Hofstede, a researcher located in the Netherlands, led an investigation that is now considered a classic in the field of cross-cultural psychology and international management. He unravelled fundamental differences between cultures regarding the ways people behave, interpret, value, or evaluate all sorts of social situations.

It started with questionnaires sent to managers in the international company IBM. The questionnaires aimed to collect information about a range of issues, including, for example, the ways managers solved human conflicts, their values, and how they thought other managers and employees should behave, etc. Over the years, this field of research grew and other researchers became involved, working either with Hofstede or independently in various regions of the globe. Data was collected in many countries, allowing the researchers to corroborate and fine-tune the developing model, which proved relevant for explaining cultural variations in many situations from family dynamics to a country's economic growth.

With results from thousands of managers all over the world, the set of data is very impressive. Statistical analysis of the results explored the relationships between answers and people according to their characteristics (such as gender, age, work level, and country). Sets of discovered correlations were grouped together. This technique, called factorial analysis, is nowadays very well known and is commonly used in exploratory research. It enables the researcher to discover which data "behave" in the same way and which participants share similar features (behaviours, attitudes, values).

Once the statisticians have done their job and extracted the groups that are statistically relevant, the psychologist's job is to discover why these data correlate and what they have in common; in other words, why certain participants end up grouped together and which of their characteristics can explain their similar answers. This is the interpretation of factors (a "factor" being a set of data linked together and extracted from this statistical analysis).

Five factors, all fairly independent of each other, emerged from this research. These five major dimensions explain most of the differences observed between people's behaviours in their working environment, in the private domain (couples, families, child-raising), and in social and political arenas. We will explore them one by one.

While reading these results, it is important to know that the differences between countries or regions described by Hofstede and other scientists indicate only average trends observed at the group level. There is much variation within places, regions, and countries, as well as at the individual level, so while I hope these statistics will help you to appreciate differences between cultures, it is important to approach every situation with a fresh mind and to avoid anticipating someone's character according to beliefs and stereotypes – including those built in by reading cross-cultural literature!

Power and Equality

The first factor found by Hofstede is the power distance. This deals with the relationship people have with authority and with social inequalities (some people having more or less power than others).

In some countries – for example, in Malaysia, Slovakia, Russia, or Mexico – power distance is high: on average, it is a common practice that the boss makes decisions, and subordinates expect their boss to give clear guidance and rules to enable them to do their jobs properly. If you come from a country with a high power distance, this might sound like a very obvious statement.

However, in countries where the power distance is lower, such as in Israel, Austria, New Zealand, or most Northern European countries, there is a less authoritarian and more consultative style of management. The boss is still the one with the power to make decisions, but there are more discussions and consultations with the employees before a decision is made. The employees are expected to take some responsibility for finding solutions; therefore, the relationship between management and employees is seen as more interdependent.

This power distance, which starts early on in life during childhood, can be observed in many other situations. In countries with high power distance, children are supposed to be more obedient to their parents; respect is required. Children tend to be more dependent on their parents because their parents are the ones who tell them what, when, and how to do things. By contrast, parents in low-power-distance countries give more freedom to their children earlier and they encourage experimentation. Children can give their opinions openly in any discussion.

In the low-power-distance countries, a good teacher is one

who helps students to develop their full potential and to find their own intellectual path. In more paternalistic countries, by contrast, the teacher is expected to have all the knowledge and to be the expert. The teachers cascade information to their students, who absorb the information like sponges, and there is little room for criticism.

According to UNICEF, in terms of child happiness (as ranked by children themselves completing well-being scales), the best-ranked country is the Netherlands followed by a range of Northern European countries. Their report does not provide an explanation, but I would bet this is partly explained by the fact that children are given a lot more freedom and autonomy in countries where the power distance is low.

In terms of scientific achievement, it is remarkable that the countries scoring the lowest on the power-distance factor – Sweden, Switzerland, Denmark, Norway, United Kingdom, Austria, Ireland, Germany, and the Netherlands – show the highest rates of Nobel Prizes per inhabitants.

Nisbett noticed that Japan had strangely low numbers of Nobel Prizes compared to the US despite a similar investment in education (the USA has the highest number of Nobel Prizes in absolute numbers; however, when compared per inhabitant, they fall just behind most North European countries). Japan was also far behind Germany, despite the fact that the investment in education in Germany is half as high as in Japan. His interpretation was that the high power distance in Japan (due to its heritage of philosophies that teach respect for older people) results in an absence of debate between teachers and pupils and, subsequently, a dramatic reduction in creativity. Promotions in Japan are not for the most inventive researchers but tend to favour the oldest instead.

Would you like to compare your home country and your host country on this dimension? Table 6.1. provides the details of

74 countries' power-distance rankings, based on Hofstede's description of the factors.

Table 6.1. Power-distance index of 74 countries and regions. The countries appear in order of highest power distance to lowest. For example, Malaysia and Slovakia with the highest power distance scores are ranked first and second, while Austria had the lowest score and is ranked last. Adapted from G. Hofstede, G.J. Hofstede & M. Minkov, *Cultures and Organizations, Software of the Mind*, 2010.

Malaysia	1-2	Belgium (Nl)	39-40
Slovakia	1-2	Uruguay	39-40
Guatemala	3-4	Greece	41-42
Panama	3-4	South Korea	41-42
Philippines	5	Iran	43-44
Russia	6	Taiwan	43-44
Romania	7	Czech Republic	45-46
Serbia	8	Spain	45-46
Suriname	9	Malta	47
Mexico	10-11	Pakistan	48
Venezuela	10-11	Canada (Qu)	49-50
Arab Countries	12-14	Japan	49-50
Bangladesh	12-14	Italy	51
China	12-14	Argentina	52
Ecuador	15-16	South Africa	53
Indonesia	15-16	Trinidad	54
India	17-18	Hungary	55
West Africa	17-18	Jamaica	56
Singapore	19	Latvia	57
Croatia	20	Lithuania	58
Slovenia	21	Estonia	59-61
Bulgaria	22-25	Luxembourg	59-61

Morocco	22-25	United States	59-61
Switzerland (Fr)	22-25	Canada (all)	62
Vietnam	22-25	Netherlands	63
Brazil	26	Australia	64
France	27-29	Costa Rica	65-67
Hong Kong	27-29	Germany	65-67
Poland	27-29	Great Britain	65-67
Belgium (Fr)	30-31	Finland	68
Columbia	30-31	Norway	69-70
Salvador	32-33	Sweden	69-70
Turkey	32-33	Ireland	71
East Africa	34-36	Switzerland (G)	72
Peru	34-36	New Zealand	73
Thailand	34-36	Denmark	74
Chile	37-38	Israel	75
Portugal	37-38	Austria	76

Now see Figure 6.3: The dotted line represents the range of power distance based on the countries where the power distance index has been studied. Find your home country in Table 6.1. and then apply it to the scale. Now do the same for the new culture you live in. You may also want to add other countries of relevance to you, for example, countries where you have lived, where your parents grew up, or where your boss is from.

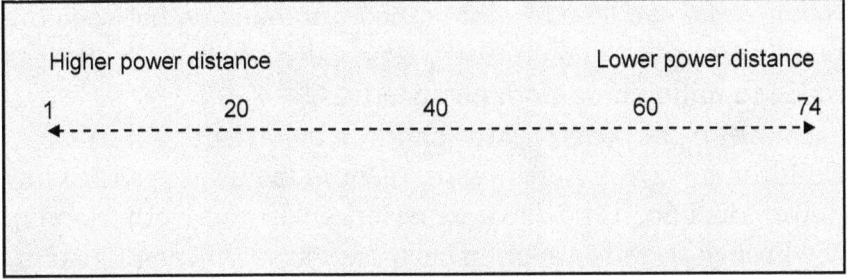

Figure 6.3. Scale representing the power-distance dimension. Fill in the ranks of your home country, host country, and other cultures you have lived in or worked in.

I have filled in the figure for myself (Figure 6.4). France, my home country, is ranked in the 27-29th position; the Netherlands, my host country, is 61st.

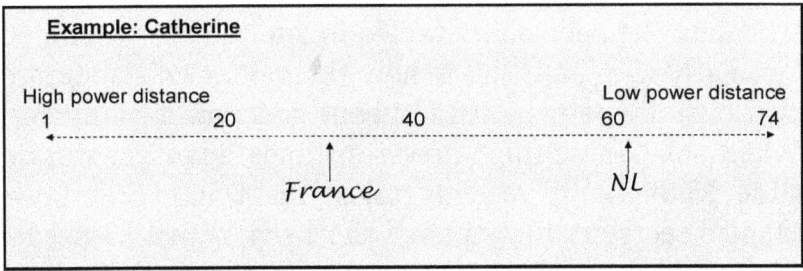

Figure 6.4. Scale representing the power-distance dimension and rankings of the author's home country and host country.

I can immediately see that, despite the very small geographic distance when viewing a map of Europe, the two countries are quite far away from each other in terms of power distance. France carries a legacy made of many centuries of domination by the Roman Empire and the Catholic religion, while the Netherlands has a very different history that led to the development of more individual freedom, less centralization of authority, and less-powerful hierarchies.

This very significant difference has many consequences in real life and can lead to a lot of incomprehension between the people from the two cultures, especially when little effort is made to understand both perspectives.

A funny example is the way children behave in public places. Children are given much more freedom in cultures with a low power distance (as I have experienced in the Netherlands). My French friends are often surprised to see "little monsters" from Northern European countries screaming in the trains or running between tables at the restaurants. However, on the positive side, this freedom gives the children an early sense of responsibility for their actions.

In France and other countries with high power distance, children are expected to behave. The adults would be afraid for their children if they were not obedient, because it would mean the children would be at risk of being unable to adapt to many situations in the future, at school and at work in particular. The behaviours valued in adult life are reinforced at an early age, and this is how the values and associated behaviours are perpetuated from one generation to another.

When a Japanese (high power distance) manager working in the Netherlands recently asked his Dutch (low power distance) secretary to prepare a short report that he needed, and she said she could not, he was left speechless. Later in the evening, he asked his wife (who reported this story to me) what she thought he should have done. He wondered if he should have her fired or moved to another department. For him, this behaviour was not acceptable. However, the secretary had probably expected him to discuss her priorities and deadlines and then negotiate or organize around them. In low-power-distance countries, people do not shy away from telling their boss about their issues in an open way. They expect open discussions. If necessary, they would say no; it is as simple as that because it is not a forbidden behaviour.

Here are some more examples from a Transition Workshop organized for parents in an international school:

> — In the UK, employees/bosses talk differently with each other than in the Netherlands where they are very direct to each other.
> a British woman

> — As a Japanese employee, I felt liberated working in the USA. I could even walk into the office of the boss!
> a Japanese woman

Observe your own results. How large are the differences between your culture(s) of origin and the cultures you have to deal with on a daily basis? Can you find situations where these power-distance differences could explain some of your culture shock? Could it explain why you don't share all of the same values found in the education system of your host country? Could it explain the attitude of your managers and your employees at work?

The power-distance dimension is only one of the dimensions that explain the main differences in values and behaviours between cultures. We will also explore four other equally important dimensions. These are represented all together in the next figure, where you can fill in your scores as you progress throughout the rest of the chapter (Figure 6.5).

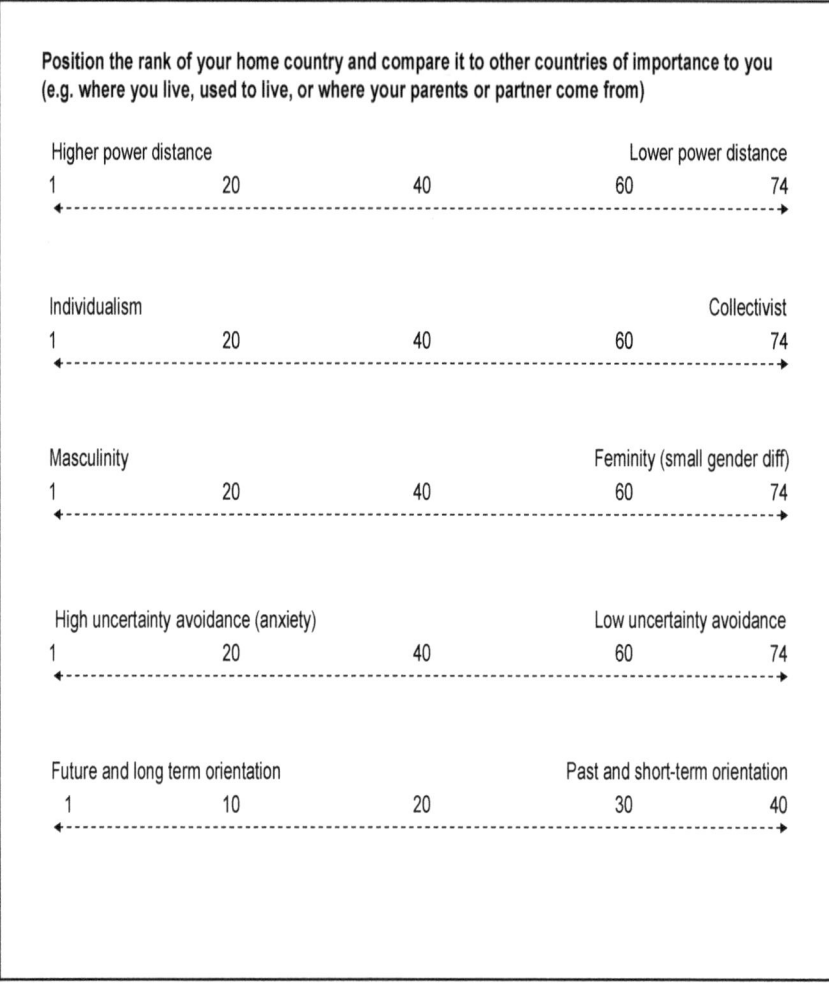

Figure 6.5. Scales representing the five dimensions of cultural differences according to G. Hofstede's model for visualising cultural differences between two (or more) countries. Report the ranks as seen in tables 6.1 to 6.5 for your culture(s) of origin and your host country.

Groups and Individuals

The second of Hofstede's factors is individualism versus collectivism. This is about the relationships between one individual and the group. Most societies are collectivist, meaning the interest of the group prevails over the interests of individuals. Societies with very high collectivist scores on Hofstede's scale are those in which individuals integrate into strong, cohesive groups. Loyalty is expected, and communities protect their members. In such societies, the family in which you are born plays an important role. It often includes very extended family (grandparents, uncles, etc.) and remains an important group of reference throughout your entire life.

In collectivist societies, social contact is quite intense, to the extent that foreigners may have the feeling that they are never left alone. Politeness is important for maintaining cohesion and avoiding confrontation (although this can be interpreted as hypocrisy by people from more individualistic cultures). Loyalty to the group is also important. There is a strong sense of shame, losing face, or humiliation in situations that have gone wrong, because being seen as a good person by the group is crucial.

By contrast, in countries with high individualistic scores such as the US and many Anglo-Saxon countries, people are not expected to rely heavily on groups: they are supposed to look after themselves and their immediate family (their partner and children). For example, children are expected to leave home as soon as they have enough financial independence. The dominant negative feeling when they have done something wrong is not shame but rather guilt. Speaking one's mind and telling the truth (being an honest person) is valued; however, a person from a collectivist society would see this as extremely rude, unfriendly, and disrespectful of others' feelings. In individualistic societies, friendship and love are freely determined by the individual and less by convention or family relationships.

When travelling to individualistic societies, people from more collectivist cultures are likely to experience distress due to the lack of social support and lack of people visiting them or inviting them out. They will find the locals too distant and difficult to hang around with. This isolation is exacerbated by the fact that individualistic people value and respect the privacy and autonomy of others: they do not want to intrude too much in someone's life or hinder another person's free action.

Table 6.2. shows the rankings of 74 countries on the individualism scale. Use this table to complete Figure 6.5 with the scores from your original culture(s) and the other cultures you have encountered, and compare the differences. Do you come from a rather individualistic country or not? Can you think about situations where you have misunderstood the values or point of view of people from a more collectivist (or more individualistic) region?

Table 6.2. Individualism versus collectivism index. High ranks (e.g. USA) indicate high levels of individualism. Adapted from G. Hofstede, G.J. Hofstede & M. Minkov, *Cultures and Organizations, Software of the Mind*, 2010.

United States	1	Jamaica	39-40
Australia	2	Russia	39-40
Great Britain	3	Arab countries	41-42
Canada (all)	4-6	Brazil	41-42
Hungary	4-6	Turkey	43
Netherlands	4-6	Uruguay	44
New Zealand	7	Greece	45
Belgium (Nl)	8	Croatia	46
Italy	9	Philippines	47
Denmark	10	Bulgaria	48-50

Canada (Qu)	11	Mexico	48-50
Belgium (Nl)	12	Romania	48-50
France	13-14	East Africa	51-53
Sweden	13-14	Portugal	51-53
Ireland	15-16	Slovenia	51-53
Latvia	15-16	Malaysia	54
Norway	17-18	Hong Kong	55-56
Switzerland (G)	17-18	Serbia	55-56
Germany	19	Chile	57
South Africa	20	Bangladesh	58-63
Switzerland (Fr)	21	China	58-63
Finland	22	Singapore	58-63
Estonia	23-26	Thailand	58-63
Lithuania	23-26	Vietnam	58-63
Luxembourg	23-26	West Africa	58-63
Poland	23-26	Salvador	64
Malta	27	South Korea	65
Czech Republic	28	Taiwan	66
Austria	29	Peru	67-68
Israel	30	Trinidad	67-8
Slovakia	31	Costa Rica	69
Spain	32	Indonesia	70-71
India	33	Pakistan	70-71
Suriname	34	Colombia	72
Argentina	35-37	Venezuela	73
Japan	35-37	Panama	74
Morocco	35-37	Ecuador	75
Iran	38	Guatemala	76

According to the 2010 Expat Survey done by the International Bank HSBC, the top emotional concerns of expat employees are re-establishing a social life (41%) and feeling lonely and missing friends and family (34%). Only next come worries about career prospects, language barriers, relocation issues, healthcare, adapting to the culture, and others.

The percentage of people who are concerned with social isolation is particularly high for expats moving to Europe when compared to other regions of the globe. Although there are language barriers in many European countries where locals do not speak English, the worst scores for "Find it easy to make friends" were from the expats living in the Netherlands, where many locals speak English fluently. The countries that scored the lowest on this question were the Netherlands, Belgium, Switzerland, the UK, and Germany.

If we refer back to the individualism-collectivism factor, the bad scores seen in expats living in Europe start to make sense. Many European countries have more individualistic values than countries in the Middle East or Asia, for example. People found it easier to make friends in Bahrain, Thailand, South Africa, and many Asian countries. There has been too little research on this topic to make any definite conclusions yet, but the results so far are both intriguing and important for the future mental health of people moving abroad. This field of research is growing and will hopefully bring us more answers and solutions in the future.

Extracts of a discussion in a Transition Workshop:

> — *I heard a Dutch lady say, "This year I will visit my mother." I thought that her mother must live far away, but I was shocked to hear that she lives in the Hague! [about 60 km or 37 miles away]*

— In Malta, we visit our parents once a week. My parents have a big kitchen where we sit and eat from 1200 to 1700 hrs. We would go to my parents and my husband's parents every two weeks.

— In Turkey, we go to our parents after our work to eat and then go home.

— In Japan, our grandparents or parents sometimes live far away, so we can only visit them once a year in the holiday. We now see that the family system is collapsing due to being so busy with work and family, having no time to pay attention to parents/grandparents. However, there are families where the daughter brings dinner to her parents every day.

— In Japan, we work for the company, not for ourselves. This is valued a lot. When I was hired for a Japanese company, I did not decide on my position; the management decided where I was working on the basis of what is best for the company. I did not mind.

Masculinity and Femininity Roles

The third factor in Hofstede's research is the masculinity-femininity dimension. This is about the differences between the concepts of masculinity and femininity, including the social implications of being born a boy or a girl, and also the acceptance and prevalence of feminine or masculine attitudes among both men and women.

In societies that score high on the femininity factor, it is accepted and valued that both men and women can be modest, gentle, and concerned with the quality of life. The tendency in feminine countries is that relationships and quality of life are more valued than earnings or status; both men and women should be modest and tender, share the same tasks at home and at work, and even share the same car. Discussions of sexual matters are less taboo, and homosexuality is better accepted as a fact of life. In schools, children are socialized to be friendly and their emotional and social development is valued. Failure at school is less of an issue because school does not value competition between children.

Countries scoring high on femininity in Europe include most countries from Northern Europe (Sweden, Norway, the Netherlands, Denmark, Finland) and some countries from Eastern Europe (Slovenia, Estonia, Russia), and also Portugal.

In societies scoring high on the masculinity pole, emotional gender roles are more differentiated. Men are expected to play a different emotional role; they are more assertive and tough and tend to focus on material success. In general, there tends to be more competition. Men are expected to compete with one another and be more aggressive than women, whereas women are expected to be more tender and focused on relationships. Women's liberation is more focused on women occupying the same positions as men at work and less focused on having men and women sharing the same domestic tasks.

Explicit discussions about sex are more taboo. There are less explicit representations of nudity, and homosexuality is less well accepted and more likely to be seen as a threat to society. There is also less tolerance for religious and cultural diversity, and religions tend to stress the male prerogative.

In the work place, behaviours will be more aggressive and more money is preferred over more free time. Politically, these societies value progress over the protection of the environment.

Many countries in Europe and most Anglo-Saxon countries score very high on masculinity. Slovakia, Hungary, Austria, German Switzerland, Italy, Ireland, Germany, and Great Britain all score very high, followed by the USA, Australia, and New Zealand.

The next table show the ranks of 74 countries.

Table 6.3. Masculinity-femininity index. High ranks (e.g. Slovakia, Japan) indicate high levels of gender differentiation and higher scores towards masculinity pole. Adapted from G. Hofstede, G.J. Hofstede & M. Minkov, *Cultures and Organizations, Software of the Mind*, 2010.

Country	Rank	Country	Rank
Slovakia	1	Israel	39-40
Japan	2	Malta	39-40
Hungary	3	Indonesia	41-42
Austria	4	West Africa	41-42
Venezuela	5	Canada (Quebec)	43-45
Switzerland (G)	6	Taiwan	43-45
Italy	7	Turkey	43-45
Mexico	8	Panama	46
Ireland	9-10	Belgium (Nl)	47-50
Jamaica	9-10	France	47-50
China	11-13	Iran	47-50
Germany	11-13	Serbia	47-50
Great Britain	11-13	Peru	51-53
Colombia	14-16	Romania	51-53
Philippines	14-16	Spain	51-53
Poland	14-16	East Africa	54
South Africa	17-18	Bulgaria	55-58
Ecuador	17-18	Croatia	55-58
United States	19	Salvador	55-58
Australia	20	Vietnam	55-58
Belgium (Fr)	21	South Korea	59
New Zealand	22-24	Uruguay	60
Switzerland (Fr)	22-24	Guatemala	61-62
Trinidad	22-24	Suriname	61-62
Czech Republic	25-27	Russia	63
Greece	25-27	Thailand	64
Hong Kong	25-27	Portugal	65
Argentina	28-29	Estonia	66
India	28-29	Chile	67

Bangladesh	30	Finland	68
Arab countries	31-32	Costa Rica	69
Morocco	31-32	Lithuania	70-71
Canada (all)	33	Slovenia	70-71
Luxembourg	34-36	Denmark	72
Malaysia	34-36	Netherlands	73
Pakistan	34-36	Latvia	74
Brazil	37	Norway	75
Singapore	38	Sweden	76

Dealing with Ambiguities and the Unknown

A fourth dimension that distinguishes countries and regions lies in their ways of dealing with uncertainties and ambiguity. In countries with scores indicating a low tolerance for ambiguity, people tend to express more anxiety and to be less comfortable with uncertainties. These cultures tend to be more expressive; for example, people in these cultures are noisier and more energetic with their gestures and facial expressions during conversations. They also show higher scores of depression, impulsiveness, and vulnerability. In general, people in these countries feel less happy and have more concerns about health and money, and family life is considered more stressful.

Because people in these countries want to avoid ambiguous situations, they tend to create structures, clear laws, and rules. Structure and directness in giving information is preferred, and they would rather take action quickly than remain in a situation where no decision is taken: they want something to happen now rather than wait for it or discuss it.

In Europe, countries differ quite a lot in this dimension. Many Southern European countries score relatively high in uncertainty avoidance or anxiety (Greece and Portugal are highest, with France and Spain at 17-22). Germany is ranked 43, which places it halfway (higher than Great Britain).

In less-anxious cultures, showing one's emotions is less well accepted. This trait can give outside observers the impression of a person who is controlled or easy-going, lazy or quiet, depending on the observer's bias. In less-anxious countries, people tend to be happier, have fewer worries about health and money, and be better able to tolerate uncertainty. They are more ready to admit when they do not know something and tend to take more risks as entrepreneurs and in their investments because they have less fear of failure.

During a Transition workshop in the Netherlands, a woman made the following complaint:

> — *In the Netherlands, once, my baby was very sick with fever. I called the doctor, and the assistant told me to wait for three days and see what happens!*

Differences in dealing with anxiety and uncertainty can generate a big culture shock at the doctor's office, as this testimony illustrates. The doctors in Northern European countries tend to have a more relaxed attitude and leave the patient in a position of uncertainty when dealing with non-life-threatening conditions. They usually prefer to wait and see the natural evolution of the disease rather than give medication that could take effect immediately and reassure the anxious patient. Culturally, in these countries, it is a very acceptable attitude, while in other countries such a doctor would be regarded as incompetent or lazy.

Uncertainty avoidance rankings by country are reported in the next table (Table 6.4).

Table 6.4. Index of uncertainty avoidance (anxiety). High ranks (e.g. Greece, Portugal) indicate high levels of anxiety. Adapted from G. Hofstede, G.J. Hofstede & M. Minkov, *Cultures and Organizations, Software of the Mind*, 2010.

Greece	1	Taiwan	39
Portugal	2	Arab countries	40-41
Guatemala	3	Morocco	40-41
Uruguay	4	Ecuador	42
Belgium (Nl)	5	Germany	43-44
Malta	6	Lithuania	43-44
Russia	7	Thailand	45
Salvador	8	Latvia	46
Belgium (Fr)	9-10	Bangladesh	47-49
Poland	9-10	Canada (Quebec)	47-49
Japan	11-13	Estonia	47-49
Serbia	11-13	Finland	50-51
Suriname	11-13	Iran	50-51
Romania	14	Switzerland (G)	52
Slovenia	15	Trinidad	53
Peru	16	West Africa	54
Argentina	17-22	Netherlands	55
Chile	17-22	East Africa	56
Costa Rica	17-22	Australia	57-58
France	17-22	Slovakia	57-58
Panama	17-22	Norway	59
Spain	17-22	New Zealand	60-61
Bulgaria	23-25	South Africa	60-61
South Korea	23-25	Canada total	62-63
Turkey	23-25	Indonesia	62-63
Hungary	26-27	United States	64
Mexico	26-27	Philippines	65
Israel	28	India	66
Colombia	29-30	Malaysia	67

Croatia	29-30	Great Britain	68-69
Brazil	31-32	Ireland	68-69
Venezuela	31-32	China	70-71
Italy	33	Vietnam	70-71
Czech Republic	34	Hong Kong	72-73
Austria	35-38	Sweden	72-73
Luxembourg	35-38	Denmark	74
Pakistan	35-38	Jamaica	75
Switzerland (Fr)	35-38	Singapore	76

Long-Term and Short-Term Orientation

The fifth (and last) dimension is the orientation towards the future, and investment in long-term objectives (for example, children's education), versus orientation towards the past (for example, maintaining values related to experience and wisdom) and shorter-term vision.

Countries scoring high on long-term orientation (or future orientation) are common in Asia, which is where this dimension was discovered and tested for the first time. China, Hong-Kong, Taiwan, Japan, Vietnam, and South Korea are the first six countries on this scale, and Singapore is not far behind. Countries with long-term orientation tend to value perseverance and sustained effort, hard work, the sparing of resources for the future, and humility. Education is highly valued, in particular, mathematics and concrete sciences; and mothers are supposed to make time for their preschool children. Old age is valued, as is openness to new ideas and learning.

Short-term-oriented countries tend to value freedom, individual rights, traditions, and short-term benefits more than other countries. For example, there is more social pressure and emphasis on spending rather than on saving money for the long term. Quick results are valued (such as monthly and quarterly results in business) as opposed to long-term investments and new ideas. Most European countries have medium scores, while the USA and other Anglo-Saxon countries (Australia, Canada, New Zealand, and Great Britain) score high on short-term orientation. Thirty-nine countries have been studied in this dimension so far (see Table 6.5).

Table 6.5. Index of short-term versus long-term orientation. The first ranks indicate a strong emphasis on long-term orientation. Adapted from G. Hofstede, G.J. Hofstede & M. Minkov, *Cultures and Organizations, Software of the Mind*, 2010.

South Korea	1	Turkey	47
Taiwan	2	Greece	48
Japan	3	Brazil	49
China	4	Malaysia	50
Ukraine	5	Finland	51-54
Germany	6	Georgia	51-54
Estonia	7-9	Poland	51-54
Belgium	7-9	Israel	51-54
Lithuania	7-9	Canada	55-56
Russia	10-11	Saudi Arabia	55-56
Belarus	10-11	Denmark	57-58
Germany (East)	12	Norway	57-58
Slovakia	13	Tanzania	59-60
Montenegro	14	South Africa	59-60
Switzerland	15	New Zealand	61
Singapore	16	Thailand	62
Moldova	17	Chile	63
Czech Rep.	18-19	Zambia	64
Bosnia	18-19	Portugal	65-66
Bulgaria	20-21	Iceland	65-66

Latvia	20-21	Burkina Faso	67-68
Netherlands	22	Philippines	67-68
Kyrgystan	23	Uruguay	69-71
Luxembourg	24	Algeria	69-71
France	25	United States	69-71
Indonesia	26-27	Peru	72-73
Macedonia	26-27	Irak	72-73
Albenia	28-32	Ireland	74-76
Italy	28-32	Mexico	74-76
Armenia	28-32	Uganda	74-76
Hong Kong	28-32	Australia	77
Azerbaijan	28-32	Argentina	78-80
Austria	33	Mali	78-80
Croatia	34-35	El Salvador	78-80
Hungary	34-35	Rwanda	81
Vietnam	36	Jordan	82-82
Sweden	37	Venezuela	82-82
Serbia	38-39	Zimbabwe	84
Romania	38-39	Morocco	85-86
Great Britain	40-41	Iran	85-86
India	40-41	Colombia	87-90
Pakistan	42	Dominican Rep.	87-90
Slovenia	43	Nigeria	87-90
Spain	44	Trinidad	87-90
Bangladesh	45-46	Egypt	91
Malta	45-46	Ghana	92
		Puerto Rico	93

Extracts from a Transition workshop in an international primary school:

> — Asian parents are more future oriented; they invest in the education of their children a lot, sometimes even sacrifice for the education. They depend on their children once they are old.

> — I've worked in India in a health programme, and I have seen that some parents who can only afford one meal a day for their entire family still save money to pay for extra lessons for their oldest child!

You can now report all your results in the general scale shown in Figure 6.5. What dimensions are very different when comparing your culture of origin with your host culture?

Cross-Cultural Knowledge

In this chapter, we have seen that many of the issues we encounter (and will continue to encounter) in social situations or with our colleagues, children's teachers, neighbours, or administration staff have their roots in deep cultural differences that were built up over centuries. These cultural tendencies were influenced by wars, economic situations, old empires, religions, climate, and other factors. Understanding them all would take more than an entire lifetime, because it's a topic of infinite complexity, but I hope this brief overview helps you deepen your understanding and discover why you may think and react a certain way in many situations, and why you value certain behaviours as "qualities" while others may consider them "faults," and vice versa.

Understanding these cultural differences better is a huge step towards adapting your own behaviour. This is not about changing yourself or your values to become like the people of the host country; it is simply about having more options: you may not like the behaviour of the local school teacher or the doctor's secretary, for example, but when you understand where it comes from, you have more freedom to react in ways that are beneficial. Rather than experiencing fury or sense of helplessness, you can discuss the issue with the teacher or secretary and find a solution that better fits your needs and values while still being respectful of the host culture's main values.

Cross-cultural knowledge is useful in new situations and, in the long term, it boosts your openness and mental flexibility. After a while, you should start to feel that you have developed an international mind-set and feel that you belong to a community much larger than the citizens of your country of origin. You will realize you are not an isolated migrant in a foreign place but a true world citizen.

The next step towards your successful cross-cultural adaptation involves developing better communication skills with locals and other internationals. We will examine this further in the following chapter.

Chapter 7

New Language and New Interactions

Researchers have observed in many studies that becoming trained in cross-cultural knowledge truly helps people to develop better coping resources. A meta-analysis has shown that cross-cultural training benefits self-development at several levels: it boosts psychological well-being and increases self-confidence; it increases cognitive skills, enabling people to develop a better understanding of host-culture systems and values; it boosts interpersonal skills during interactions with host nationals; it increases a person's ability to adjust and show the new behaviours expected from the host culture; and (also important) it boosts work performance. So what will help you or hinder you in your interactions with locals or strangers?

— Get out and get involved. Learn the language, join local clubs, like sports clubs, be open to culture and people, don't hang on to preconceptions and stereotypes.
Mike, raised in England, Ireland, and five states in the USA, five years abroad as an adult (the USA, the Netherlands)

— Do as much research as possible before arriving in the country and try to learn some of the language.
Simona, English,
six years abroad (the Netherlands)

Starting Point

Not everybody is equal, and you should be aware of your starting point. Three factors influence your ability to develop cross-cultural knowledge and cross-cultural communication skills as well as how quickly you develop these skills.

First, it depends on your experience with travelling and your knowledge of the new country. Have you travelled and settled in other cultures before? Have you already stayed in the new country for a long time? Have you decided to stay in the country, or do you intend to leave in a couple of years? All experiences accumulated before and during our stay, as well as our willingness to stay, help us to develop the mind-set of openness, patience, and motivation that enables us to adapt better. If you have already lived in other cultures, perhaps in your childhood, you probably learned to avoid being too judgemental towards a new culture. You may have learned to like other cultures and probably developed a good awareness of cultural differences in behaviours and values.

Second, you can learn a lot about the local culture, both indirectly and explicitly, from workshops, books, or websites dedicated to cultural learning in general or to the local culture in particular. The more knowledge you gain, the better and quicker your adaptation.

You must do your homework by reading and learning about the local situation and a little bit of the geo-politics, and it helps if you explore the region during weekends and holidays. Invest time in gaining some notions of the history, the political situation, the economic and business drivers, and the main societal issues.

Finally, the quality and the number of contacts you have with the host culture will tremendously influence your adaptation: the more and the earlier you are in touch with the local culture and local people, the better your knowledge and intuitive understanding.

Learning a New Language: Pros and Cons

When I started to work as a psychologist, my first job brought me to a school for children with sensorial deficiencies. It was my first encounter with deaf children. I found Sign Language lively, expressive, and visually very beautiful. Sign Language has a grammar, a rich vocabulary, and visual poetry. It is a true language. However, outside their special classrooms where teachers spoke Sign Language, most deaf children lived in hearing communities and hearing families. This meant they could not detect most of the messages in their natural environment. Mute your TV for a few minutes and watch the interactions of the people on screen, and you will gain some idea of what the world looks like without sound. By not having access to the auditory content in their environment – from the news on TV to all the informal conversations surrounding them – these children missed out on an enormous amount of information. In addition, because of their difficulties in understanding oral language, they also struggled to learn to read.

As such, they needed a lot of detailed explanations and other forms of information to compensate for what they could not access easily from their environment. Some children had developed false beliefs based on their many misunderstandings of the surrounding world. For example, some thought they would never be adults and would die before reaching adult age because they had never seen a deaf adult.

In a way, foreigners who arrive in a country where they do not speak the language can experience similar isolation from information. A French woman who arrived in the Netherlands with her husband and two young children told me that she felt deaf and mute after her arrival because she could speak neither Dutch nor English. We arrive in a very silent world if we cannot understand the local language. The beautiful movie from Sophia Coppola, *Lost in Translation*, shows this sense of isolation in the two main characters who are Americans staying in Tokyo for a few days. It illustrates how we can end up being surrounded by crowds and yet still feel very isolated, as if we were deaf.

To break the silence and start to adapt, it is essential to learn the local language, or at least to learn some of it. Start as soon as you arrive. I learned Dutch when I arrived in the country but only at a very basic level, and after this my level did not progress for several years. Now I consider this a mistake, although back then I had many other worries and priorities. I did not invest in learning the next levels because it was hard work and costly, and I did not have much money. Also, most Dutch people are fluent in English, so I worked on my English rather than on my Dutch language skills. I also had bad memories of learning German at school, and I believed we would leave for another country soon enough. The list of real or imaginary obstacles was a long one. Do you have as many excuses as I did?

My avoidance of the language became a problem a few years later: we did not move, and after two years in the Netherlands, my work contract ended and I had to find a new job. In retrospect, I should have learned the language earlier, had a diploma validated, and prepared myself for another career; but instead I had just carried on without seeing the obstacles that not speaking the language properly and not having done enough networking would create.

I am not extraordinary: many internationals stay for much longer than they planned. One day we are expats or internationals, and then, before we know it, we have become a settled immigrant with no particular intention to leave.

Richard, a UK citizen, arrived in the Netherlands ten years ago. It was only for a short-term assignment, but the international company he worked for sold his division: "I was sold!" he said. "I lost my return ticket!" He had to learn the local language. At the time of writing, he is working in a company where most people around him speak Dutch. His wife, also from a foreign country, had to learn Dutch too. They have not given up the idea of living somewhere else in the future, and their two children are enrolled in an international school, but they are also now fluent in Dutch and have taken up hobbies that require use of the Dutch language.

What happened to me next? After several years in the Netherlands, I could speak Dutch well enough to buy a couple of things at the market: "Please give me that fish there. Yes, head cut. Thanks!" My market-Dutch language abilities were not very useful in other places (and no, I do not ask to get heads cut off very often, even though I am French!).

After several years, I decided that I needed to resume language classes and really make an effort to learn the language. My motivation this time was much greater. This is all it takes, really. It made my life so much easier and made me feel so good about myself. I could regret that I did not do it earlier, but we all learn as we go along, and there is only so much we can do; regrets are not really helpful. The lesson here for me was that it is never too late to start, but the most benefit comes from starting as early and as intensively as possible.

Learning to understand and speak the local language (or one of the languages spoken in the host country) brings you a huge advantage. It will have a very strong impact on your adjustment and enables you to avoid being (and feeling) isolated. It allows you to communicate on a daily basis with all the people in your life (not only the other expats) and to learn about what is going on in the society around you. In particular, it opens access to the local media and gives you some social competence: a personal knowledge and awareness of the place you are walking in. If you know the gossip and the things people are worrying about at any moment, you can take part in the small everyday conversations. The topics may not be vital, but knowing about them helps you to feel connected. It feels good to exchange a few words with your neighbour in the morning, even if what you say is not so important.

Although it takes a few months to reach a good intermediate level, once the motivation is there it is not as hard as you might remember from your school years because the language surrounds you every minute, at least if you allow it to. There are various ways to learn a language, and you can choose to learn and speak about what interests you the most. In contrast to the school situations you may have experienced as a child, this time you are in charge. Understanding the local culture and a new language gives you a strong sense of achievement because you know you have mastered your situation and your environment.

Extracts from discussions during a Transition Workshop in the Netherlands (note: for most participants, English was a second language):

— I live in the Netherlands and I do NOT speak the language; and I am proud of it! My husband did not encourage me because, he said, "We are not going to stay in this country anyway."

— My life changed when I learned Dutch; I got a better position and got more power to learn.

— If you do not know the language, you live in a bubble: the TV is Dutch, theatre pamphlets are in Dutch. Once, my girlfriend took me to the theatre for a musical; it was in Dutch and I did not understand a thing!

— I took my American children to a playground to enjoy playing and meeting new friends. I saw them playing at first, but then they were sitting in a corner, crying. Back home, I asked them why they were crying. They told me that there were children asking them "Hoe heet jij?" [In Dutch, this means: "What is your name?" but it sounds like the English, "Who hate you"]. My

children misunderstood; they thought the children told them, "We hate you."

— My child came home from school singing a song, "The wheels on the bus go round and round." I did not speak English that well at that time, and "bus" means "shit" in Finnish. I punished my boy for saying this wrong word!

When you arrive in a new country, learning the local language sounds like the logical and straightforward thing to do for many, but some internationals strongly disagree with this. There is not a right or wrong position on this subject because we do not have such simple lives and learning a new language, which is expensive in time and money, may not be on your priority list. Many expats ask themselves whether it's worth the time and money or whether they should try to find a compromise and invest just a little in language learning. They may wonder which language is most useful to start with, or wonder whether it's worth the effort at all. Here are stories and opinions from internationals and expats:

— Mexicans do speak English, but the majority not very well, so you have to learn the language. So when I was in Mexico, I had to improve my text book Spanish. Basically, I taught myself because I could not afford classes.
Edda, Dutch,
nine years abroad (Israel, England, Scotland,
Mexico, Turkey, Greece, England)

— I already knew French, and although I did attempt to learn Wolof, the local language, I did not succeed. But with French, I can communicate with almost everybody here as it is the national language.
Sandra, Swiss,
six years abroad (the Netherlands, the USA, Senegal)

— In Bangladesh, I tried [to learn the local language] but [it was] too difficult. In Africa and in France, I learned to speak French

from scratch and was fluent after a while. Language has never been a huge barrier for me.

Marieke, Dutch,
eight years abroad (Bangladesh, Benin, France)

— *I need to learn this $%^&*#@ language!*

Sarah, US citizen,
four years abroad (Ireland, the Netherlands)

— *Yes, I am in the process of learning Dutch, because it is important if you want to feel at home and more important for my research so that I can interview those who cannot speak English or are more comfortable in Dutch. It is also the native language of my mother, who unfortunately during my youth did not teach me the language.*

Julia, Canadian,
two years abroad (England, the Netherlands)

— *In Uganda, English is the official language of conduct. However, only educated people (having finished at least primary school) speak English. The rest of the people speak a local language, varying greatly between regions. I felt uncomfortable expressing myself in English initially. I remember that I was exhausted during the first one or two weeks because of this language effort.*

Karen, Dutch,
six months abroad (Uganda)

— *I did learn the local languages. It is the lowest bar that has to be taken in order to feel comfortable in new society.*

Andrei, Bulgarian,
seven years abroad (the USA, Spain)

These stories show us the many different situations and many different reasons to learn the local language, official language, or dominant language... or, if it suits you, to avoid learning any new language and instead survive with the languages you have already mastered.

In many cases, the true expat only expects a short stay, so they ask themselves why they should learn the local language. Millions of internationals also find it more urgent to speak English rather than the local language because English is the most common language in their new international community. They may need English, rather than the local language to be able to interact with colleagues or school teachers. Learning English may be the logical first step, leaving the local language to be learned at a later stage during longer stays.

Some people have a particular emotional attachment to a language because their parents or grandparents emigrated from the country where it is spoken. They may have a higher motivation to learn and master the local language. In other cases, in countries where the local language is hardly spoken outside of the country, the motivation to learn it is generally lower than it is for countries where the language is more widely spoken, such as in the case of English, Spanish, Portuguese, or French.

> — *I have a student who is from Eastern Europe, and she said the first language she learned in the Netherlands was Turkish! This is because the only job she found was a cleaning job in offices; her new colleagues were all immigrants talking in Turkish and so she had to learn it in order to be able to talk to them.*
> A Dutch language teacher in the Netherlands

> — *[Question: Did you learn the local languages?] Shamefully, no! I did try while in the Netherlands, but the nature of my social relationships and later my work did not allow much room for practice, and I was still building and perfecting my English. I can still recall some words and can read the newspaper headlines, but that's about it.*
> Cintia, Portuguese,
> eight years abroad (Brazil,
> Netherlands, Dubai the United Arab Emirates, Singapore)

— At the start, no [I did not learn the local language], because my priority was to be able to communicate to my husband's colleagues and also because we were not supposed to stay more than three years. I also feared, rightfully, mixing up both languages. And also, one year after our arrival, I became very sick and I had to make choices. After that, I was very busy with my job where I need to communicate in English. So I still take [English] classes. In terms of budget, you also have to make choices. But this situation is very frustrating actually. So last June, I started to take Dutch classes. I took a two-week intensive course, and it helped me to put into practise all the things I've learned passively for all those years.

Sandrine, French,
twelve years abroad (the Netherlands)

Although there is no clear answer to the question of which language to learn, some languages are more common and some are easier to learn. If you intend to travel again later, it is more rational to learn the dominant languages.

According to the Ethnologue.com website, 6% of the world's languages (about 390) have at least one million speakers and account for 94% of the world's population. By contrast, the remaining 94% of languages are spoken by only 6% of the world's people. Obviously, some languages are very dominant and it is more logical to learn those unless you are an ethnologue, a linguist, or an anthropologist. It is almost a necessity to learn English when you are planning to travel abroad and meet with expat communities.

Your ability to learn a new language does not depend much on your general intelligence or memory skills. It seems that everybody can learn a language. It is simply a matter of effort and motivation. However, not all languages are equally easy to learn. An important factor influencing your ability to learn the new language and also how quickly you can learn it is the distance between the languages you already know (your native language or a second language learned at school) and the new language.

This distance can be evaluated according to each language's

historical roots. Languages evolve, and populations encounter each other or disconnect from each other due to migrations and wars. As people move and as their new environment changes, so does their language, including their grammar and pronunciation. New words, often borrowed from encounters with other cultures, appear, while others disappear because the population does not need to use them anymore.

For example, many technological words borrowed from English have entered the vocabulary of various languages due to technological developments (online, in several languages, we "tweet" or "google" things). On the other hand, as old jobs disappear, the names and verbs describing the activities and the tools involved disappear with them. If you have lived abroad for some time, you may even have had the experience of visiting your home country and discovering new words and new expressions that did not exist before or that had a different meaning when you were still living there.

Among the many large families of languages from the past, the proto-Indo-European language is thought to have been at the origin of the many languages now spoken in Europe and Eastern Asia: the Germanic languages, Latin languages, Indic languages, Iranic languages, Celtic languages, and others. Their similar features are due to their common linguistic roots.

English and Dutch, for example, used to be one language, which at the time was neither English nor Dutch but a common proto-language: the proto-Germanic language. Having the same ancestor language, English and Dutch still share many grammatical features in common, and many words look and sound very similar.

A practical consequence of the shared histories of different languages is that you will observe some people in language classes learn much faster than others. This is usually due to their previous knowledge of similar languages (of course, there are also some people who do their homework, and some who don't... but all else being equal, language roots matter a lot). For example, I met a Chinese woman who tried to learn English and Dutch as soon as she arrived in the Netherlands, but as she had never learned any Indo-European languages before, she struggled much more than the English speakers who were also learning Dutch. When you can speak English, you will find it easier to learn Dutch or German than would a Spanish, Italian, or French person who has never learned any Germanic language before. Inversely, learning Italian, Spanish, or Portuguese is much easier for a French speaker than it is for speakers of Germanic languages. Likewise, most native languages in Pacific Asia or Sub-Saharan Africa are difficult to learn for Indo-Europeans.

On the next page, the language tree illustrates the roots of Indo-European languages (Figure 7.1). It shows the proximity of languages and their common roots. Languages that share common roots, especially those that only diverged from their proto-language recently, still have many words, phonemes, and grammatical points in common.

This should not be an excuse for not trying to learn a local language, but when other people around you seem to find it easy to learn the language or seem to be learning it more quickly than you, do not get discouraged. It might be that they are already familiar with the grammatical structures or can recognize similar words, while for you the language structure is completely new and thus difficult to memorize all at once. Rather than be discouraged, use your knowledge about proto-languages to motivate you to learn, because learning one foreign language will help you tremendously in learning other languages with common roots.

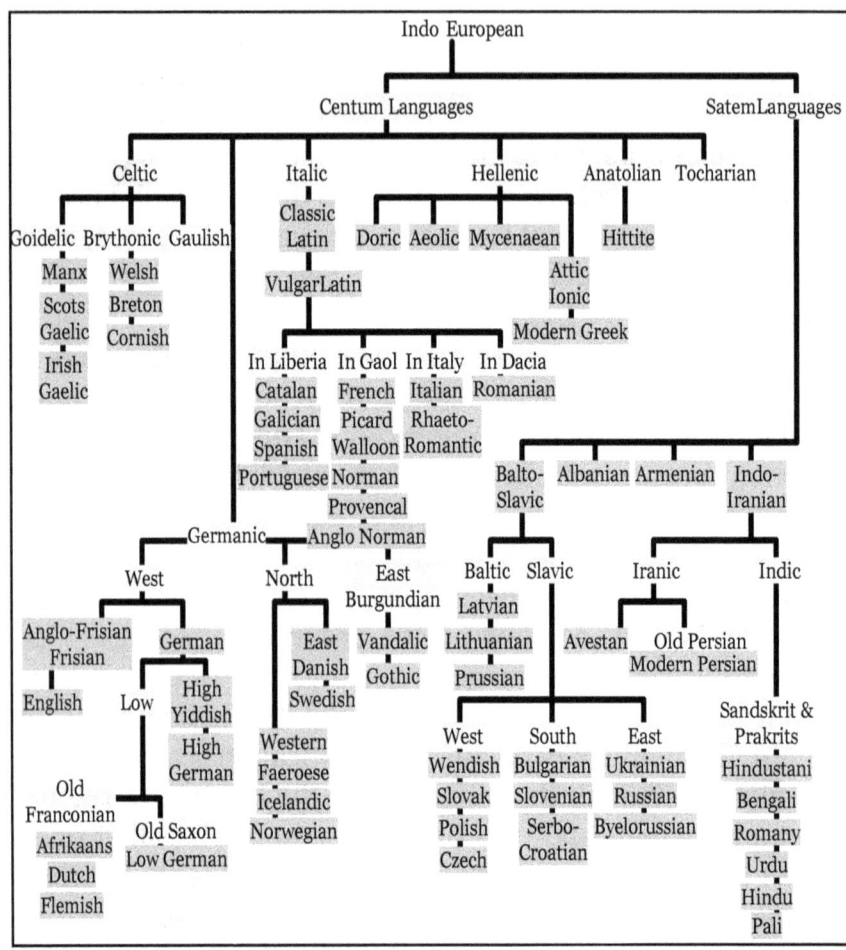

Figure 7.1. Roots of the main Indo-European languages. Languages with roots that are closer in time have evolved more recently from a common proto-language and therefore share many similarities in their vocabulary, phonemes, grammar, and syntax.

Realistic Expectations

Learning to speak a language takes a lot of effort, time, and discipline. You may have to spend several hours of study every week for months if you want to become fluent. Learning the language in the country where it is spoken means you have intensive exposure to it, which greatly facilitates your progress. Still, you cannot learn it passively. It requires a conscious effort right from the start.

According to many studies that have examined the varied memorizing techniques you can use, making the effort to retrieve the information after it has been learned is the most efficient way of memorizing new words and new phrases. You can do this by learning lists of words and phrases. It is the most tedious method, but it works. Personally, I try to create short imaginary dialogues with the new words I have learned, even though this can be very difficult to do in the beginning.

There is a critical period in life for learning a language, after which many people struggle to ever totally master certain features of the language. When a second language is learned after the age of about nine, even after several decades of practising it on a daily basis, the speaker will retain a little of their original accent and will make some grammatical mistakes that a native speaker (or a person who learned the language before the age of nine) would not make. This means that if you learn a language as an adult, you should relax a little and be realistic: you will always have a foreign accent to some extent and you can count on missing some grammatical subtleties.

This occurs even when learning Sign Language. Studies conducted in people aged fifty- to sixty-years old who were not native signers but who learned Sign Language after they were nine years old and practised it daily for decades showed that they still had a sort of "hearing accent" in their hand gestures, which native signers do not have. Therefore, retaining an accent has nothing to do with your mouth or tongue. Past nine years old (or around this age), there is simply less flexibility in your brain to learn certain aspects of a language.

However, there are other aspects of the language that you can learn without any age barriers: the ability to learn new vocabulary is tremendous and does not seem to be significantly reduced after a certain age. Children learn a lot of vocabulary during their childhood. They are exposed to school learning where many new concepts are thrown at them. If, as an adult, you put yourself in a similar position and spend some time every day learning a new language, you will also be able to learn several new words a day – certainly not as many as a toddler would but enough to build up a large vocabulary in only a few months.

If you practise regularly, the new words will be kept in your memory more easily. It is important to be exposed to these words regularly. The more you hear or read them, the better you will be at remembering them. Whether you start learning to speak English at age fifteen, thirty, or fifty, as long as you continue to use it a lot, read many novels, and expose yourself to activities where you need to learn new words, your vocabulary will soon be as good as a native speaker's.

To motivate yourself (if you need to), keep in mind that the first weeks of learning a new language are the most tedious: you need to learn new phonemes (vowels, consonants, intonations, and pitches), which are hard to hear and to pronounce, along with all the new and basic grammar rules you cannot ignore (word orders; expression of present, past, or future tense; genders; and numbers, etc.).

But after the basic and new aspects of the language are learned, you enter a phase where all you need to do is continue to learn new words and practise them, thus avoiding forgetting the words you have just learned. You can fine-tune, of course, and be willing to learn much more, but this is not necessary to achieve fluency. This is the most rewarding phase of learning a language, because you can learn by talking to people, by watching TV or movies, and by starting to read magazines. At this stage you start to enjoy it because your new language skills enable you to learn about your new environment without limits.

Of course, it is a long and sometimes frustrating process: you learn a new word... but then you forget it... you encounter it again and learn it again... and inevitably forget it again. But since you are in the country and do not have an exam to pass, there is no need to panic; you will see this new word again and again, and after a few times you will remember it easily – and even automatically – without much effort anymore.

Are you too old to learn a language? You may have heard that we progressively lose some of our brain flexibility with age. In fact, this loss is extremely slow and accelerates only at a very old age. Besides, these changes affect only a proportion of the population. Many people age very well and maintain excellent learning skills throughout their life, especially if they have trained their brain to learn continuously and if they often expose themselves to novelty. Learning new skills is part of a healthy lifestyle, together with physical activity, eating well, and community involvement. So a mature age is a good reason to start to learn a new language rather than an excuse to avoid language classes.

Non-Verbal Signals

Situations in which cultural differences are noteworthy can lead to misunderstandings, frustration, or anger. Scientists have observed many sorts of interactions that can go wrong, and there are many elements of these interactions that expats should be careful about. These elements go beyond the verbal exchange.

The following list covers the most important cultural differences in communication and offers tips on how to identify and handle certain situations. Look out for these types of differences during your interactions and ask locals questions to better understand the dos and don'ts.

- Many routine communications are ritualized, for example, ways of greeting or leaving. Pay attention to the conventions or rituals at the start and end of an interaction; the rules and etiquette, such as punctuality; and the ways to accept or decline invitations.
- The conventions in verbal communication may involve more than just saying the correct word: it is often not enough to learn to say only "yes" and "no." For example, Asians have various ways to express "no" without saying it too directly to avoid conflict. Listen for how to make an apology or say "thank you," because it might involve saying more than one simple sentence. Westerners who are unaware of these subtleties can seem blunt and brutal by some cultural standards.
- Carefully observe the voice, silences, length of speech, and intonation. Listen carefully to the voices: observe whether people around you tend to speak loudly or softly and listen to how they make requests or show respect by changing the intonation of sentences (the rising or falling of their voice at the end of the sentence). Become aware of the silences during meetings and dialogues: some cultures accept that people will try to talk all at once with enthusiasm, while other cultures encourage people to take turns during interactions and subconsciously signal this with short silences after they are finished speaking (as is the case in the Netherlands, at the lunch table, for example; it was something I found difficult to adapt to).
- English can be misinterpreted, especially between a native speaker and someone using English as a second language. A classic example in a working environment is when you say, "Would you like to..." or "Could you please..." to give an order. It can be taken literally and

lead employees to reply "no" because they think you are giving them a choice rather than an order.
- Most idiomatic expressions are difficult to understand for non-native English speakers. The first time someone told me she was "having a bad hair day," I looked at her hair and thought it looked as usual; however, she meant she had had a bad start to the day.
- How you address someone (for example, whether to use the formal or informal "you" or their formal title, or which name to use first) and how you interact with them (for example, at what point you can exchange business cards) is important. These rules of etiquette are usually taught by your language teacher. If not, watch and listen carefully to what most people around you do.
- Body language is tricky because it is not something we usually think about consciously while communicating. However, as you get used to interacting with other cultures, you will develop a strong sensitivity to the non-verbal signals sent to you. As a teacher in an international school said to me, "We develop antennas."
- The way expressions such as smiles or frowns are used varies a lot between cultures. Negative facial expressions may be difficult to detect in cultures where people smile a lot by convention. Westerners can think that Chinese people are hypocritical because they smile all the time, making it hard for Westerners to know when they actually disagree. It takes some time to develop the ability to detect the subtle differences in Asian smiles.
- The level of mutual gaze used (i.e. the frequency of eye-to-eye contact during a verbal exchange) can also lead to misinterpretations: some cultures are high-gaze, a behaviour which can be perceived as a threatening or intrusive by people from low-gaze cultures; inversely, people from low-gaze cultures (who prefer to avoid direct eye contact) can be seen as not paying attention or can appear dishonest to others.

- The conventions for how men and women should interact or distance themselves from each other differs greatly between cultures. Learn about these differences and remain very aware of the appropriate way to behave in the new culture you are living in.
- Personal space, the space one person must give to another out of respect and so the other feels comfortable and unthreatened by the interlocutor, also varies between cultures. People in some cultures typically stand closer to each other than people from other cultures, and some are used to more body contact than others (for example, during greetings and informal situations).
- Gestures do not travel well: they vary greatly and can have very different meanings in different cultures. Before you have learned them, it is safer not to use gestures involving fingers – you have been warned!

The best way to learn quickly is to keep your eyes open, ask questions, and learn from your mistakes. Most internationals have stories of misunderstandings caused by non-verbal communication or have done something wrong while trying to be nice and friendly. It is just part of the learning process and is usually a good reason to laugh at ourselves afterwards!

Understanding Other's Intentions

While cultural habits blur communication between strangers, we are nevertheless well equipped to perceive each other's intentions and, to some extent, to feel each other's emotions. Beyond the cultural ways of saying, doing, and showing, there is something universal we can strongly rely on when we want to communicate and build trust, form meaningful relationships, or pursue love or friendship with people from different cultural backgrounds.

In the early 1990s, a fundamental discovery was made by Italian researcher Giacomo Rizzolatti and his team from the University of Parma: they discovered mirror neurons.

Neurons are the brain cells responsible for transmitting information to and from the body as well as for generating consciousness. Rizzolatti's team monitored macaque monkeys in certain situations and observed the macaque's neuron reactions when they did or saw things. When an animal makes a movement, very specific neurons fire. What the researchers discovered was that neurons from the exact same region fired when the macaque's merely observed another macaque's, or even humans, making the same movement with similar intentions (such as reaching the arm out for food). This was a major discovery.

Before this, scientists had assumed that we "think" about other's emotions and intentions. This discovery indicated that, instead, animals *experience* other's intentions almost directly. Mirror neurons, so called by the researchers who discovered them, were found in very specific areas of the animal cortex. A few years later, another research team confirmed that mirror neurons exist in humans as well.

It seems that when we see another person "has something in mind," we are detecting this information because our mirror neurons are playing a simulation of that person's emotions or intentions directly in our brains. Rather than say that we "understand" another person's emotion, it seems more appropriate to say that in many cases we "feel" their emotions: we experience the same changes in our bodies as the person we are looking at, and we translate this into feelings (our interpretations of these changes).

The discovery of mirror neurons was an important milestone for social neurosciences. Mirror neurons, which give us the ability to read other's expressions as signs of their internal states, were critical for our evolutionary survival; they enabled us to develop social lives. Thanks to mirror neurons, we can feel and guess other people's intentions and emotions.

When we experience this with another person, our feeling of bonding with them is very strong. Although cultural habits can sometimes lead to misunderstandings and blur the messages, as seen in Chapter 6, the fundamental cognitive and emotional ability to read people's intentions is automatic and universal.

From here, we can imagine that mirror neurons might be the basis for empathy; however, this has not been clearly demonstrated. Empathy is a highly complex function because it involves not only how we feel but also how we respond. In particular, it involves emotional regulation in order to control the effects of emotions and to produce the appropriate responses according to the context. The result is that we are able to build strong connections with people who were initially just strangers. This is what we will now explore.

Chapter 8

From Strangers to Friends

We are social animals. Our species has evolved and survived over millions of years because of our ability to live together in small or large groups, raise our children together, and organize our security and food-sharing. Socially supportive relationships are essential to our well-being, physical health, and mental health. In this chapter and the next, we will see why social bonds help us to remain mentally healthy, and we will learn how to build a strong network of friends and acquaintances in a new place.

The Health Benefits of Connectedness

In cross-cultural studies, it has been shown that strong social support reduces physical and mental illness during sojourns abroad. The health benefits of connectedness are a universal phenomenon. Hundreds of studies have shown that socially involved persons are happier and healthier and live longer than socially isolated people. The magnitude of the association is such that the mortality risk associated with social isolation has been compared to the negative effects of cigarette smoking, whereas the positive benefits of social involvement to physical health have been compared to the benefits of physical exercise. Supportive relationships also protect individuals from a multitude of mental health problems, from mild depression to suicidal ideas.

The amazing effects of social support on health are not yet fully understood by scientists, but several ideas have been suggested to explain the strong association. One is that social support might lower stress and boost the protective effects of the immune system. Studies on patients with immunodeficiency and other studies examining the immune response after a vaccination showed that stress-reduction therapies involving social support (group therapy) have a positive impact on biomarkers of stress. However, the chemical mechanisms underlying such effects are still largely unknown.

Social integration provides the basis for a strong sense of identity, stability, and self-worth. Although it is difficult to define and measure the meaningfulness of our lives, it seems that social support is associated with a sense that life is worthwhile. People report a greater meaning in life when they have someone to live for, such as children, a spouse, and family.

Another benefit of family and friends is that they can also directly influence us towards healthier behaviours, for example by saying, "You forgot your seat belt," or "You should really stop smoking." Naturally, social networks can also sometimes have a negative influence; for example, having friends and colleagues who smoke makes it harder to quit smoking. However, the positive impact of social support and social involvement outweighs its negative influence.

Perception Biases

Our impression of how much interpersonal support we get is almost as important as the support we actually receive in reality. Indeed, sometimes our perceived support does not correlate with our actual support: we can have the feeling that we are without much support when in fact it is there, but perhaps not fully adapted to our most pressing needs or simply not noticed.

In times of suffering, our perception of support can be seriously impaired. For example, we may feel that people around us cannot find the words to comfort us. In spite of the support objectively received, it is possible that we perceive our needs are still not being fulfilled. It is also possible that our social support is temporarily weak. The people who usually support us psychologically may be dealing with their own emotions or their own suffering.

Nevertheless, we often receive a lot of invisible support. Most of the time, we are so used to getting support in everyday situations that we start to take things for granted, forgetting the cost to others. A spouse who financially supports a family or who prepares the dinner every evening can eventually be perceived as not contributing enough. Routine kills the appreciation of what others do for us.

We have to keep in mind that our perceived support depends on us. This will enable us to be happier by appreciating our blessings and by communicating to others that we appreciate what they do. This can be surprisingly difficult, because we are wired to become habituated to our situations and to do or perceive things in automatic ways once they become repetitive.

In an international company where English was the official working language, I heard locals complaining how hard it is on them to have to speak another language in their own country:

> — Sometimes, there are nine of us in the room, but there is just one foreigner, and we have then to speak in English just because of this person. It is hard.

Before hearing this, it had never occurred to me that the locals saw the obligation to speak in English as a service they provided for us foreigners working in an international company in a non-English-speaking country. After all, English may be a foreign language for the international workers as well. This is a form of support I was not aware of until I talked openly about my frustration with the language issues with a colleague, a local who had never lived in another country. The conversation was an eye opener for both of us.

There are plenty of similar examples of support we do not notice all around us. Once we start to pay attention to them, we become more aware of the efforts others make. It feels good to realize that we actually get a lot of invisible support. We are not as alone or as left out as we may think.

Social Support Awareness

Social support is present in many forms. There is, for example, emotional support when people express that they care for us and try to comfort us; informational support when people provide information, advice, and guidance; tangible support when people help us materially; and social support when a sense of social belonging is built by sharing social activities (for example, by going to a concert together).

Are you aware of the support you receive from others? Try to find five examples illustrating how locals, visibly or invisibly, support you. Think about neighbours, colleagues, or perhaps the server at your favourite delicatessen. Do they speak to you more slowly because you are a foreigner? Do they help you with paperwork? Are they resourceful when you need to know where to find something? Can you go out with them just for fun or to discover the region? Take some time now to write down or just think about five examples.

After you have made your list, turn your attention to another type of network and find five other examples of support you receive from other migrants, expats, and internationals. Think about material help, comfort, entertainment, practical information, and sharing emotional issues.

If you took the time to complete two lists and found several good examples of social support, then your awareness of the help you receive has been raised. You will feel closer to the people around you who have shown you a lot of generosity by offering their time, effort, money, or empathy when needed, whether or not you asked them for this. Enhancing your gratitude towards people in this way increases your feelings of connectedness. This is a simple way to add new positive feelings to your daily life and to help you reach the 1:3 ratio of positive experiences recommended by Frederickson for establishing good emotional well-being.

Open Up to New People

We all (without exception) tend to be attracted to people who look, think, and behave like us. Psychologists call this phenomenon homophily: "homo" refers to the same, and "phily" to the attraction. Homophily drives how we choose our friends. In a foreign place, we have to break this mental habit to some extent or it will drastically reduce the number of friends and even acquaintances we make. We must learn to see strangers as potential friends in spite of their superficial differences, and we must learn to discover people's qualities independently of their appearance, accent, or social origins. We must also forget about any stereotypes we hold about certain cultures and countries.

If you are a woman from the UK, married and with children, and you expect to meet other married women from the UK in a different country, you might go to clubs where such women meet. However, the chances are high that you would never have become friends with these women had you met them back in the UK. By contrast, if you enlarge the range of people you talk to, you will find many people – men and women, people from different countries, some married and some not, some with children and some without – who happen to share more in common with you in terms of values, personality, and the things they love doing.

You may discover they share the same passion as you: they may sing in a baroque choir or row in a club nearby, or they may have just registered for a Sushi workshop. Or perhaps they will prompt you to realize something you only vaguely dreamed about before meeting them. They may also inspire you to try out something new you had never thought about doing or never knew existed. These things happen because you are exposing yourself to more diversity than you did before.

If you come from a background where you had little exposure to other cultures, this may feel frightening, because you may not know what to anticipate when you meet people who are rather different from you. You will wonder how you should behave and what you should say.

Studies have found that we can reduce our fears about strangers by simply thinking about what we might have in common with them: romantic love, love for children, caring for ageing parents, or worries about money, health issues, and pain. Feelings of love and pain are universal, and you can rely on the most basic but most important things all humans share to feel close to others, even in the most remote places.

As you get used to meeting new people from various cultural backgrounds, you will discover that behind the differences, most people have the same needs: the need for connection and love from others, and the needs to feel safe, to feel appreciated, and to have a good laugh. Our worries and sorrows are the same as well, from worries about health issues and financial uncertainties to the terrible pain that follows a separation or the loss of a parent, child, sibling, or best friend.

During my interviews with internationals, those who had travelled in several countries and lived abroad for several years told me they had developed the ability to make friends relatively quickly. They said they were more open in their communication, less inhibited by the social norms (the "what will people think?" worry) and acted more spontaneously. Social pressure is reduced in international circles, which will help you develop your skills at connecting with new people, and you may soon find that you enjoy it a lot.

Avoid Stereotypes

We interpret behaviours based on automatic processes, but sometimes we have to un-learn certain ways of thinking because the automatic attribution of causes can seed the roots for misunderstandings and stereotypes.

The problem with humans is that we think a lot. We interpret. We generalize. We cannot stop finding causes and consequences. This mental capacity has very useful functions in most cases. On the positive side, if we find out why something happens, the world seems a more comfortable place because our knowledge allows us to predict what will happen next. The quicker we can anticipate events, the quicker our responses. Our brain has evolved to think about the world as a place where there are categories and certain rules governing things (e.g. an apple falls down from a tree; it will never fly up). These rules give us knowledge we can rely on (if you shake the tree, the apples will fall down and you will have something to eat).

In a situation involving a person's behaviour, and in a perfect world, the same would apply. If he smiles, he likes something – and perhaps it is you; if he frowns, he does not. But in a situation with a stranger, these automatic rules do not always work. If you are a woman and a man is talking to you and looking you in the eyes, this could be interpreted different ways: if he is from a culture where this shows directness, it is the norm for him, but you may interpret this as flirting if you are from a less-direct culture. If you interpret the situation automatically and base your interpretation on your own cultural references, the chances are great that you will misinterpret his behaviour.

The problem is, you have been using many implicit rules of causes-consequences throughout most of your life, so you are interpreting the situation and making associations between his possible intentions, emotions, and behaviour without being aware you are interpreting these at all. It is your automatic mode.

These automatic processes are further biased by another phenomenon. Social psychologists have unravelled a classic bias that occurs when people interpret other's behaviours. To start with, in most situations we tend to attribute our own behaviours to different causes than we would if the same behaviour were observed in another person.

For example, imagine that a colleague you don't know very well arrives a bit late to a meeting. Most people will tend to think it is because that person is lazy, negligent, or disorganised. An alternative interpretation could be that he had to drop his kids off at school and could not do it earlier. Both explanations are equally possible, but in the first case the explanation makes a general negative statement about the person, whereas in the second case the focus is on the circumstances.

In the same situation, if you were the person who arrived late, you would more likely think that your delay was due to some external circumstances such as bad weather rather than personal flaws (such as being lazy, negligent, or disorganized).

This important bias is technically named the "fundamental attribution error" by social psychologists. When things go wrong for us, we attribute it to external circumstances (and not so much to our flaws), and when they go right, we attribute it to our good qualities (luck or circumstances tend to take a secondary role). However, we don't extend this courtesy to others; we too easily look to blame them personally.

Racism and stereotypes against some groups of people (whether they are Irish, Arab, Californian, blond, gay, Republican, left handed or tax officers) develop because of what psychologists call the "ultimate attribution error." It is a cognitive bias that has been observed in many situations.

The ultimate attribution error happens when we observe an individual who belongs to a group we hold a stereotype about and then we attribute his or her behaviours to a specific cause that reinforces our stereotype. If the person does something good but we have a negative stereotypes about their culture (for example, we think all people in this culture are lazy), then we will tend to think their example of good behaviour is an exception due to circumstances rather than evidence of their positive personal qualities. If the person does something of which we disapprove, we use it to reinforce our negative stereotypes: "I knew it! They are all the same."

In other words, the ultimate fundamental error is to think that when strangers from a different culture do something bad, it is because that's the way they are, while also thinking that if they do something good, it is circumstantial due to external reasons or because they are simply unlike the others. When thinking this way, the stereotypes remain intact and the world in our mind remains stable and predictable. If we do not have mental flexibility and aren't able to change our categories (e.g. who is good, who is bad), this leads us into keeping our stereotypes.

Does this bias actually exist in all cultures, or are we less biased when we come from certain parts of the globe? It seems that people in collectivist cultures tend to blame circumstances more than do people from individualistic cultures, where explanations tend to take the form of personal attributions. So, in fact, collectivist cultures tend to make fewer errors of attribution. This is bad news for the Western world, where strong individualistic values augment the risks of developing strong group stereotypes.

How does this bias develop and change with frequent exposure to cultural differences? Most internationals become more flexible and more open-minded after travelling in very different cultures. Their assumptions have been challenged, and they start to make different attributions, even without necessarily being aware of it at the start. They progressively develop more tolerance and mental flexibility in social situations.

Unfortunately, I have also observed the extreme opposite and have met quite a number of internationals who were very critical of the culture in which they lived. Some admitted to me that they hated the culture in which they had found themselves. One woman who had moved from the UK to a nearby European country told me she was sorry but she had become "racist" (in her own words) against the locals; she just could not stand "them" – even though she had a few good colleagues among them whom she saw as exceptions.

— *Pushing my boundaries, looking at other people and living things through different lenses has given me a flexibility and creativity in approaching the situations that wouldn't be possible if my paradigms had not been broken.*

Cintia, Portuguese,
eight years abroad (Brazil, the Netherlands,
the United Arab Emirates, Singapore)

Postpone Interpretations

To avoid false interpretations and biases in your judgment, especially when you are in the heat of conversation, suspend your interpretations for later. Observe and listen more than you talk, and stop thinking so much. A very important quality to develop when communicating with locals or foreigners is to be able to remain calm and open-minded, even when the situation becomes quite unclear. Learn to deal with uncertainty. When we know the explanation for certain behaviours or events, we are less anxious, because the world seems more predictable and we can guess what people will say and do. To deal with uncertainty and unpredictability is to deal with quite strong fears.

For example, if you tell some colleagues a joke at the coffee machine, you would expect people to laugh and to tell other fun stories, or simply to smile and recognise that your intention is to be friendly. When things do not happen according to plan – when nobody laughs at your joke or when people make unpleasant faces in response – it can be very disconcerting, upsetting, and to some extent frightening. Now what? you think. What will happen next? How can I achieve what I want here? How will I ever be liked or be recognised as a good colleague and good employee?

If you are not able to deal with a certain level of anxiety, you will look for direct explanations. Nobody laughed at your joke because their sense of humour is not subtle, you will think. Or perhaps they are stupid, or they do not like you. You may conclude that they probably do not like people from your country. And here you go! You are holding on to your stereotypes. Alternatively, you might think they did not laugh because your joke was stupid or because you are the idiot. Such self-depreciation is also a very destructive interpretation. This time you have turned your negative thoughts against yourself.

Having to hear people laughing about something you do not understand is truly painful, and not being able to share a simple laugh with other people can be sad and frustrating. We discussed what rejection feels like in the chapter dealing with loneliness: it creates physical pain. However, despite the pain, you should let it go and not rush into destructive interpretations. Use the ABCDE technique here again. Perhaps it's simply a language issue and people did not understand you? Most likely, it is because jokes and humour are not universal. Humour is partially dependent on your nationality, culture, and origins.

The reason we all have this cognitive bias and rush to interpret behaviours so quickly is that our interpretations make our situation more predictable, which makes us feel safer and gives us a sense of mastery over certain situations. We create a mental paradigm that makes it possible to predict what will happen next and what we need to do.

In the example above, we might decide we should stop making jokes or stop trying to be friendly, but the chances are very high that we would be wrong in our interpretations. We had the illusion that we understood the situation, but, in fact, we were probably far from the truth. If we reacted automatically, our world could become even more difficult to interpret, not simpler. We would not be stronger because we did not learn how to adapt for the next time, and on top of that we may have developed new stereotypes or nurtured old ones.

We may even accuse others of having stereotypes themselves. We risk losing self-confidence and spiralling downwards into self-depreciation.

You need to accept that sometimes you just do not yet know the explanation. Living in uncertainty for a moment, or for a few hours or a few days will leave space for you to change your ideas and question your own paradigms and behaviours. Reports from individuals who were confronted with a very different culture and were successful in understanding it often describe situations where they had to keep an open mind and not jump to interpretations. The explanations come after a while, when you ask questions. However, save questions for later when you are not feeling too emotional or frustrated, and if possible ask these questions of the people you have learnt to trust.

Build Trust and Intimacy

Ultimately, communicating is about feeling good and about feeling part of something larger than just yourself. A successful communication is collaborative, or contingent. It involves building trust. It is built on the ability to feel what the other person feels, as well as the ability to communicate about one's own feelings.

Harry Reis, a researcher from the University of Rochester in the USA, has done a great deal of experimental research involving the systematic study of people's interactions. He asks participants to keep diaries of their everyday communications, including the type and quality of the relation, over several days. Participants must interrupt their everyday activities and take notes as they occur. It is an interesting approach, because research is often based on opinions expressed much later, which are easy to collect via short questionnaires but are less precise than information taken immediately following the events.

Based on a large amount of data, he developed the theory that intimacy is reached when three conditions are met: 1) one person expresses self-revealing thoughts and feelings; 2) the partner responds to it in a supportive and appropriate way; and 3) this response is well received. This pattern does not necessarily happen in one conversation, nor does it happen regularly or every day, but as a general rule and over time the partners alternate between the two roles of self-disclosure and listening. When partners feel this intimacy, they experience very positive emotions, such as the feeling of being understood and the powerful feeling of belonging to a whole that is larger than themselves. It builds a strong intimate relationship that satisfies both persons.

It is less easy to develop intimacy and use disclosure with locals. It is, however, surprisingly easy with other internationals, because many are familiar with being in touch with other cultures and are accustomed to having brief relationships with people. They have learned to make friends here and now. Building intimacy with people with little experience in travelling may feel a bit more awkward. However, "people are people," as one expat woman wrote to me. With some care for the other person's feelings, some compassion, and some empathy, everything should go well.

It is also important to listen to the other person carefully. Being a careful listener involves asking questions to deepen our understanding without being intrusive or annoying or taking too much of the other person's time. It is a fine balance. For all conversations with strangers, try to ask for information from the other person to check whether you understood them correctly; for example, rephrase what was said to check if this is what was what they meant.

It also helps to observe how others interact and to ask

for advice from friends who have lived in the country for a long time. You might ask how they deal with their personal relationships, what values are important to the locals, and what are the most disrespectful things you should avoid. Never stop asking questions. Truly respect and try to understand the differences between yourself and the other person.

In Western countries, extraversion is a plus in interpersonal relationships, but it is not universal. In the Western world, extravert people have more friends and will feel more relaxed in interpersonal situations. Extraversion is even trained in some programmes to help people build more resilience and more self-confidence. However, in most other cultures, extraversion is not necessarily a good thing. A study conducted of English-speaking expats in Singapore showed that extravert personalities suffered more from boredom, depression, and poor health than introverts there. In Asian cultures, discretion and modesty are more highly valued, and extravert behaviours are less appreciated.

Ask For Help

Helping others is one of the keys to finding happiness in life. It satisfies one of our most fundamental psychological needs – social belonging – and gives us the wonderful feeling that our life is meaningful, which in turn is very fulfilling. Recent studies show that when adults or children are given the opportunity to show empathy, share a small amount of money, and offer a small gift to others, their mood is lifted. They felt happier than the people in the control groups who were not given the same opportunity.

Asking for help is another matter! This feels very uncomfortable to us in most cases because it impairs our sense of freedom and our desire to manage our issues ourselves (this has to do with our needs for autonomy and competence, as discussed in-depth later, in Chapter 10). However, helping and getting help are two sides of the same coin. You will not be able to start helping others if you do not benefit from other's help. Accepting the help of others will greatly facilitate and accelerate your integration. You need to look for it, accept it, and, of course, show your appreciation to the persons or community who helped you.

You will probably find it uncomfortable to have to ask basic questions. Your feeling will oscillate from slight discomfort to supreme humiliation. When we arrive in a new country, we need so much information and help from others that it is truly annoying and even exhausting to have to keep asking for help or information. It is a frustrating situation to ask from others again and again, because it doesn't feel equal. When we are in a situation where we need help and have few opportunities to help others, it may remind us of our dependence when we were children.

In the book *Strengths in What Remains*, Tracy Kidder tells the true story of young man named Deo from Burundi, Africa. He survived the civil war opposing Hutus and Tutsis and arrived in New York with two hundred dollars that had been sent to him by a distant cousin. He had nothing else, nobody to contact, and no way to get food or a roof over his head.

In the book, Deo describes the terrible humiliation and frustration of having to go and ask for help, to get medication, to find a place to live, and to find solutions to his many issues. He keeps returning to a church where a lady working for the rectory provides him with information and support. He feels terribly ashamed, but he is trapped and sees no other solution than to keep asking her for help. Before this, in his country, he was a medical student who treated patients. Now he is a war refugee who has little food, takes on an under-paid job as a delivery boy, can hardly speak English, and sleeps in a park at night. He describes feeling like a child due to being so dependent on others. Being too proud to accept help would have prevented him from rising above his pitiable condition, but in fact he is able to seek help from some amazing people who help him get back on his feet, follow his dream, and eventually help many others in need.

There should be no shame in asking for help and taking it when needed, because it leads you on the path to one day being able to help others, in your own way, using your new strengths and your own resources. The alternative is to stay in your apartment (let's hope you have one) and not asking for any support, but this would mean you could not progress much. First, get some help for yourself in order to sort out all your issues, and then you will be in good shape to contribute to your new communities.

Chapter 9

Integration and Support Networks

As foreigners in a new country, we meet people on our path who, because of their diverse cultural and linguistic backgrounds, are very different from our acquaintances and friends back home. Less visible but just as important is the new types of communities or networks these people are part of: these are new social structures to which we have only few or no links.

Finding our place in the new social system is vital. Strong networks and social support influence our well-being and physical health in the long-term, help us fulfil our need to belong and be appreciated by others, and help us to achieve our objectives by providing emotional and material support and information.

It is essential to understand how to enter into new networks, how to find your position in the new social situation, and how to build and consolidate your networks in the new place and in your new role.

Optimal Adaptation

Voluntarily or not, we develop our own way of "going about our life" in the acculturation process. John Berry calls this an "acculturation strategy": the pattern of new behaviours and attitudes that migrants adopt towards the host culture and towards their culture of origin. Will they, for example, adopt new ways of eating, wear new types of clothes, and celebrate local festivities? And, at a deeper level, will they modify certain values or attitudes and start to think and act like locals? Will they be influenced in the way they raise their children? Or will they avoid contact with the host country people?

An acculturation strategy is about how we continue our life while adapting to the new situation. It depends on the situation and on our own objectives. However, some strategies will lead to personal growth and will help us find a role in the new social environment and networks (for example, at work, at school, or in the neighbourhood), while others will not help us to build appropriate and strong coping skills and will more likely to result in suffering and isolation.

Researchers have classified acculturation strategies into four categories, depending on whether the main influence comes almost exclusively from the culture of origin (separation) or the host culture (assimilation), or from both (integration), or from neither (marginalization). The acculturation strategies are illustrated in figure 9.1.

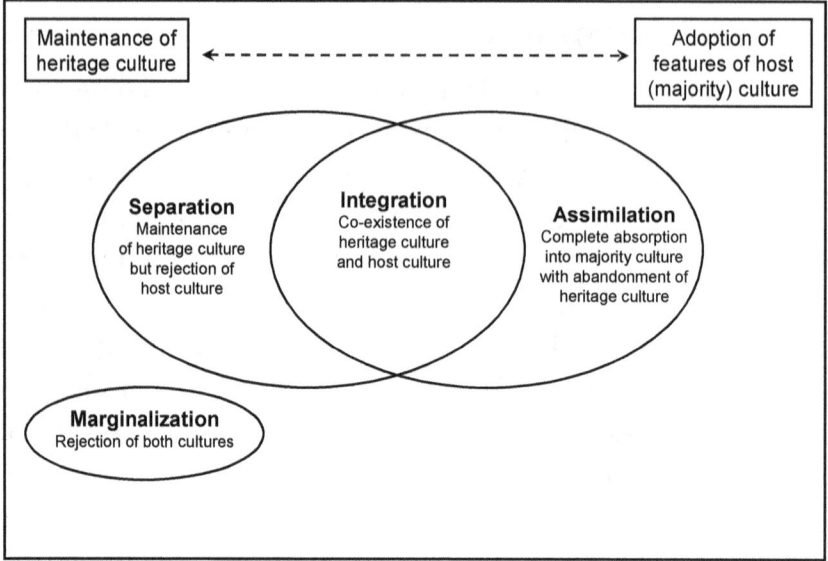

Figure 9.1. Four types of acculturation in migrants (freely adapted from Berry's acculturation model).

The classification of acculturation strategies into four types has been used for immigrants settling permanently in a country, so it does not always totally fit with some of the situations that expats and internationals encounter; however, the insights it provides are important. This approach has enabled researchers to discover how the links or absence of links with the local and dominant culture and with the culture the person is familiar with (in the model, the original culture) impact health. Scientists have measured the success of these four adaptation strategies on well-being, physical health, and mental health. This is not an abstract model of what life should be like based on philosophical or political theories but rather a model based on data collected in various countries and communities by a diverse range of researchers all studying the impact of immigration on health.

A number of studies in immigrants showed that the

integration strategy (links and ties with both cultures) was associated with better outcomes than the other types of adaptation strategies. The immigrants who adjusted to the host culture while maintaining ties to their own cultures in terms of cultural identity and social links had the best scores in terms of well-being, physical health, and mental health. This was true for immigrants from various regions of the globe, though little data is available for non-Western countries.

Separation and assimilation lead to poorer scores. Separation occurs when the foreigner rejects or is rejected by the host culture and builds up little or no social network in that culture. Assimilation occurs when migrants make an effort to adapt to the majority culture, albeit at the cost of their own culture.

The worst case is marginalization, which occurs when people do not make an attempt to adapt to the new culture (or their attempts fail) while also being isolated from their ethnic group and their roots.

However, things are slightly more complex for internationals or expats who live in between at least three cultures. First there is their culture of origin (which can be further complicated if they were raised in multiple countries); then there is the local culture in the country and region where they live (although this may be the most unknown just after arrival, it is the culture that prevails and dominates at work, in the media, in the stores, and in cultural life); and third is the international or expat culture, with English most often as the international language (though there are many exceptions).

Very often, internationals arriving without any ties in the host country make friends within international environments as a starting point, before they begin to understand how things work in the local life. When the local language is not English, the international culture becomes the place where English speakers meet spontaneously to find support. Non-native-English speakers will often learn English before the local language and also join these groups.

International networks start from encounters in international workplaces, meetings with colleagues and their spouses, and in international schools, clubs, support groups and meeting groups. On-line forums and websites for expats and internationals are booming (the definition of an "expat" or "international" varies, so it's worth checking both terms when you do an Internet search). These forums or websites are a quick and easy place to start finding information in English, and they can lead you to venues for international social gatherings in your town.

Figure 9.2 shows an attempt to fit the third culture into Berry's acculturation model. This is not a theoretical and validated model but an ad-hoc illustration of the types of situations that can be found. Some situations are similar to Berry's description of immigrants' situations; however, many situations are much more complex.

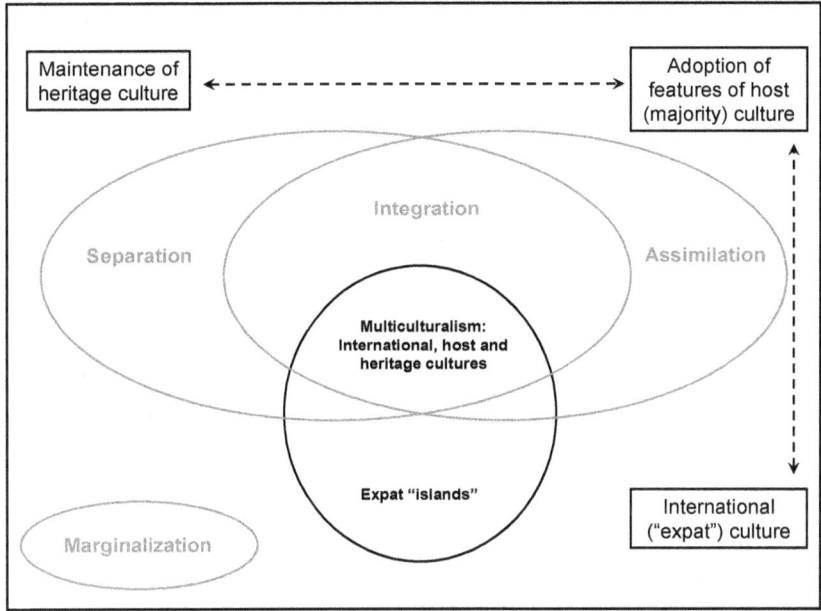

Figure 9.2. Hypothetical model adding a third dimension (international or expat culture) to Berry's acculturation model.

Integration as the Optimal Adaptation Strategy

Integration is the most successful acculturation strategy in Berry's studies. Integration occurs when the migrant maintains cultural integrity (the culture of origin) and also seeks to be part of the larger dominant network in the dominant culture of the host country. Several studies show that having strong links to one's own ethnic group has a very positive influence on mental health. Some authors have discovered that integration is associated with reduced levels of mental disorders, depression, anxiety, cardiovascular problems (resulting from chronic stress and feelings of helplessness), and fewer cases of drug addiction.

One of the important messages of these results is that it is very important to be pro-active and build new connections with new social groups, both with the locals (or indigenous) and one's own ethnic group.

Can we say that, for internationals, the most important thing is to maintain links to one's own culture, or are the links to the international culture equally or more important? There is no clear answer. The research suggests that it is important to build links with people who have foreign origins, probably because they can provide the type of support that locals cannot. They can share information and emotional support, because they have experience with acculturation and with finding their way in the country as foreigners. You can relate with them more easily because you share the same problems and the same experiences, such as culture shock, issues with administration, and the ups and down in your emotional life. Internationals also tend to develop openness and curiosity, which make it easier to connect with each other.

I asked internationals, "What would you recommend to a best friend to help him or her cope with the stress after arrival?" The answers below are very helpful and illustrate the acculturation of internationals who, consciously or not, chose the type of successful integration recommended by the immigration literature.

> — *Every move abroad or not abroad is stressful, but it passes so you have to see beyond that, and in our case we had the support of the company, and you just need to use that support in every way possible. However, if you do not have the company providing you with help, you have to inform yourself (preferably before your move) and do research so you know where to start, who to call, what to do, etc., etc., in order to settle in properly. Find out if there is an expat network in the city you are moving to and join them. There are people there who can help you because they have been in a similar position, so they know what it feels like. Plus they have lived there already so they know the ins and outs. If there isn't an expat network, you have to ask your colleagues or, if you are an expat's wife/husband, you ask your husband/wife to ask his/her colleagues. Or you ask the mums at school,*

in case you have children or volunteer. Conclusion: my advice is not to be shy and ask, ask, ask whomever. There are always nice people around.
Edda, Dutch,
nine years abroad (Israel, England, Scotland,
Mexico, Turkey, Greece)

— Take the most information you can before departure: cost of the local life, the nice areas for living, the schools... ASAP, meet other expatriates. It helps to talk about your doubts... and also to receive the most information and help that you can. For example, immediately I met a neighbour who explained to me where is the good bakery, which day is the local market, and recommended an electrician... some stupid things like this help a lot.
Marie, Belgium,
four years abroad (Brazil)

— Try to interact as much as possible with the locals, and, if possible, with people that are in the same situation as you are. This way, your integration will be quicker and you will, at the same time, be able to put things into perspective.
Myntje, Dutch,
one year abroad (South Africa)

— Do not close yourself in, but invite others, or go out to meet them. Understand that you are not alone in your feeling (other foreigners may feel the same). However, it is also just a period everyone will have to go through. Accepting that and focusing on the positive points also helps. After a bit of time, you will get used to the culture and start adopting it as well (relatives back home may be surprised!!).
Marieke, Dutch,
eight years abroad (Bangladesh, Benin, France)

Adopting an integration strategy where you spend time associating with other internationals or with people from the same origins as yours will not impair your efforts to fit into the local culture. This is counterintuitive for some people. Some internationals I spoke with tried so hard to fit into the new culture that they consciously avoided cultivating their own roots or developing an international identity. They chose another type of acculturation strategy, assimilation, which is slightly less successful for reasons I will explain now.

Assimilation and the Limits of Trying Hard to Fit In

Assimilation is the acculturation strategy of immigrants who do not wish to (or sometimes cannot) maintain strong links with their own culture. They try to fully adopt the new culture and act like the indigenous (local) people; they become like one of them and seek out many interactions with the local culture.

This is very common and often happens when immigrants choose to positively settle in and embrace the local culture as their own. They may reject their own culture in an effort to forget the past and may do their optimal best to fit in and avoid discrimination. Sometimes the host culture does not really give them a choice and exerts a strong pressure for people to fit in; it may not tolerate certain cultural differences. However, there are more difficulties and illnesses reported among people who adopt this strategy when compared to those who choose integration.

In international groups, it is a rare strategy because of the nomadic lifestyle of most internationals. Sometimes, internationals are not sure how long they will stay in the same place, although they may commit to several years. In this situation, some try their best to fit in, even though they are almost certain they will leave after a few years. They force themselves to restrict their contacts with international communities or expat communities from their original country because they think (wrongly) that it will help them to adapt better or quicker. For example, they may choose to live in a village with almost no other foreigners around them.

Many do this because they are enthusiastic about settling

in. They have a strong will to fit in and to truly experience the culture from inside by immersing themselves in it. Sometimes they do it because their spouse is a local and they think this will help the adaptation become quicker and smoother. These motivations are very positive drivers; however, many of the people who try to assimilate in this way report difficulties in adapting:

> — I still suffer from homesickness. I do not think I will ever belong here. Because I chose to live in a Dutch-only neighbourhood, I feel even more isolation. In retrospect, I would have lived in an expat area to make myself feel more engaged with my neighbourhood, to make more friends.
> Sylvia, USA,
> four years abroad (the Netherlands)

> — I'm very lucky that I have my husband but, apart from that, I have made almost no friends in the Netherlands apart from a few very nice colleagues. I deliberately decided (wrongly) to not join any expat networks as I did not want to cut myself off from the local Dutch people, but, with hindsight, I now realise that this did not work.
> Simona, British,
> six years abroad (the Netherlands)

Indeed, it is necessary to start early and work intensively to fit into the host culture, for example by learning the language and courtesy rules, learning the history and religious background, and sharing in the traditions, festivities, or social events. But cutting the bridges from internationals or co-nationals in the host country will not help this. Networks of migrants and internationals can help you in ways the local people cannot: local people may take things for granted and have less time and less interest in investing in new friendships. They are busy enough, and they already have plenty of friends, family, and neighbours. Also, they will not fully understand what you are going through or how much support you need when you arrive. Only those who have experience with settling abroad will know how difficult this can be and will intuitively understand your needs and provide you with useful information, so it is important not to restrict yourself to one group or another.

Another reason why restricting yourself is not the best strategy is that you could lose the special richness of character that comes from incorporating your own culture into a new one. Your cultural background makes you unique. It is part of your identity, and people from many other cultures may be interested in your culture of origin and ask you for information. You could miss out on this enriching experience if you do not enter into an open-minded environment where cultural differences are appreciated.

Also, it would be a shame to try to fit into a new culture without enriching it with your own knowledge. Being and feeling international opens the door to an infinite amount of knowledge from various parts of the globe, and discussions can become extremely interesting and rich.

Having a strong sense of identity can help you maintain strong self-confidence. On the other hand, comparing yourself to locals may lead to a loss of self-confidence. You will never know their culture, habits, language, who is who, etc., as well as a native, and you will never be able to compete with locals in many domains. They have a better mastery of the language than you, have many more social contacts, know about the laws and how to get things done, and have more access to media. Therefore, your strength is exactly what you may see as your weakness: your different cultural background is your richness, and locals, especially those who have never travelled, lack this aspect of character.

Use and develop this strength to grow and enrich your knowledge, mental flexibility, and creativity. Don't try to deny or erase your cultural background because you feel you must dedicate all your energy to trying to fit in with the local people; instead, celebrate both cultural influences in your life.

Separation and the Limits of Co-national Support

The "separation strategy" describes immigrants who settle in a country but make friends mostly with people from their own culture, sometimes giving birth to entire ethnic communities that hold onto their original culture and avoid interactions with the host culture. This type of strategy in immigrants leads to a withdrawal and is not the most appropriate strategy especially when your stay might be for several years. However, sometimes immigrants feel this is their only choice.

I met a Dutch man who complained that his wife, a Chinese woman, did not adapt to the Netherlands because she was spending most of her time with Chinese friends and would not learn the language, although they had been living in the country for about six years and had a child there. They did not intend to move to China or elsewhere, so his expectations were that she would learn the language, meet Dutch friends, and have a "normal" (Dutch) social life.

She probably found integrating into Dutch culture very difficult while finding it easier and more natural to find friends that shared her own language. Chinese people had formed a large ethnic group in their town, and this is where she naturally went to meet new friends and join a community. This was clearly a separation strategy (using John Berry's model), as it separated her from the dominant Dutch culture. It created a lot of tension between her and her husband because their social life was reduced to a minimum (according to her husband) and there were consequences that affected their child's education.

Many internationals choose a separation strategy because it better suits their needs. If they expect to move to another country after a few months or years, they may be cautious about spending too much time and energy learning about the culture, learning the language, or even building friendships with locals. It is also common to end up living in cities or communities where the international culture is dominant: they only meet with other internationals and have little, if any, contact with the local culture.

> — In Dubai, we felt that it was not that easy making friends and meeting new people. Maybe because it is a melting pot and there isn't really a dominating culture, people tend to socialize within their own linguistic or ethnic group – even at lunch for work, people will not go out per department but rather per nationality: Egyptians with Egyptians, Indians with Indians, Pakistanis with Pakistanis. Being a Portuguese in that context, I did try to join some of the groups, but language and habits immediately became barriers that made the whole experience unpleasant. I literally started to introduce myself to any Portuguese speaker and finally organised a party at my place to invite all of them… from there, there was a natural choice regarding who would become closer friends. But it worked really well and some of them we are still in touch with.
> Cintia, Portuguese,
eight years abroad (Brazil, the Netherlands,
the United Arab Emirates, Singapore)

Cintia, from the example above, is a truly international person who made an effort to learn about her host culture in Dubai, but she encountered an environment that did not enable her to meet much with the local people. As most of her neighbours and colleagues were also expats, she tried to integrate with the international culture, but this strategy did not work either. She was flexible and started to adopt local (international) habits by inviting people from her own culture to socialize with her. This was not an attempt to withdraw from either the host culture or the international culture but a temporary adaptation that enabled her to make friends rapidly. Cintia has moved six times in eight years, so there has not been much time to adapt to or learn about each culture. She has become flexible and quickly adopts strategies that help her accomplish what she considers the most important: making friends quickly and getting help from them to settle, get information, and find her way.

According to Berry's classification, this is a separation strategy. Although it is not recommended for long-term stays, in this particular case it is a good adaptation strategy because Cintia and her family will not stay for more than two years, her work does not require contact or knowledge of the locals, and, when some of her attempts failed, it allowed her to bounce back and try a new approach to building a network of friends and acquaintances.

The separation strategy is also popular when entire communities of internationals live in the same geographic area that is totally isolated from the local life, in particular for security reasons such as in expat compounds. In a compound surrounded by security barriers, the host culture, which is the dominant culture outside the compound walls, is not present. In terms of adaptation to the host culture, it is of course a hopeless strategy, but adaptation to the host culture is unlikely to be a priority for people living in the compound.

One interesting question this raises is whether it is detrimental to health and well-being to live amongst only a narrow set of acquaintances. There has been little research on how strongly living in isolated expat communities affects health. On the positive side, some expats living in those conditions report having a lot of fun in this life. A temporary settling in an expat compound with few external ties can be a perfect place to very rapidly meet new friends and feel part of a community where neighbours help each other and organize outings together, and where children knock at your door every day to play with your children. Networking can then take place extremely quickly compared to a situation where you are left alone, perhaps without a job or single acquaintance, in a big foreign city.

However, very small networks like these are typically places where contagious beliefs or negative emotions (sometimes collective hysteria) can take place. One expat who lived in such a closed world for two years reported to me that in the beginning, she regularly attended "coffee mornings" organized by spouses; however, these circles were somewhere the housewives openly criticised their husbands, their husband's absence, or men in general, along with many other things, including the company that was paying for their luxury life. She reported that under this negative influence, she started to have couple issues. Once she realized what was going on, she was able to stop this activity and avoid spiralling down into negativity.

Another issue arises when expats live in luxury compounds and work for the local population who lives in poverty. Voices of the Poor, the poverty group led by Deepa Narayan, systematically interviewed thousands of people living in the poorest places of the globe. They reported that one of the main failures of charitable and UN organizations working for developing countries is the lack of real understanding between the poor and the helpers. Cultural and language issues are not the only issues then: security is a major concern for expats and prevents a smooth integration within local communities. There is fear and mistrust on both sides.

Finally, some people settle abroad but deliberately restrict their friendly interactions to co-nationals. Co-nationals are a strong source of support and easily give us a sense of belonging. Just the simple fact that you are free to talk in your own language and share the same cultural references helps to diminish stress and feelings of powerlessness and alienation. However, if this becomes the exclusive source of support, the co-national ties will alter your chances of engaging with the dominant local environment. In groups of co-nationals, there is sometimes too much commiseration and criticism, which can lead to a "sinking ship" morale.

Studies done on Africans living in the US and British living in Australia show that there is less integration and more dissatisfaction with some expat groups who spend most of their time with compatriots and have fewer host national friends. Such groups can become a place where it is permitted and encouraged to criticize the host country and to develop nostalgia and unrealistic idealization of the home country. Members of these groups often discourage others from engaging in local activities. If someone attempts to say something positive about the host country and its people, they may be laughed at, ignored, or ostracized.

Generally speaking, it is preferable to avoid being dependent upon only one type of community or cultural environment (or network, as we will see next).

Marginalization and Worst-Case Scenarios

Many people have too few interactions with people from the host culture, international culture, and with people who live in the host country but come from their native culture. They follow a strategy of marginalization. Studies show is the worst of all in terms of health and well-being outcomes for immigrants. This strategy is very detrimental to mental and physical health. Sometimes, people can follow the marginalization strategy in the very first weeks of their arrival but later adopt a new strategy. However, when marginalization becomes permanent, it can be extremely debilitating.

> — *My first expatriation was in Bangladesh, and I was twenty-one years old. I did not dare to go out by myself for the first three weeks, because everywhere I went, fifty people were following me. The work environment was totally new to me (as a student), and I did not get a lot of support from my supervisor. In the first three months I did not have friends of my own (I was too shy to go towards others), and I had difficulty in integrating in the institute I worked (with whom to eat at lunch?). I felt totally lost at work and had to force myself to get into a riksja in the*

> *morning to go to the office.... After three months, I started to have more of a social life.*
>
> Marieke, Dutch,
> eight years abroad (Bangladesh, Benin, France)

Marieke, from the sample above, soon overcame her initial fears. At the time of writing, she is in her forties and has a leading role in international projects that help to fight malnutrition in the poorest regions of Africa and Asia.

> *— I keep in touch with my old friends by Skype, but the ties got thinner with every year of my staying abroad. Recently, almost only virtual contacts are kept, except one real in Delft.... To deal with this, I structure my day, plan activities for the younger kid to be among people and kids of her age, and take her places to meet someone. Pretending I have at least someone to invite for a birthday party, I organize activities, since even the artificial friendships based on some short-term common interest are better than nothing. I learned the way of socializing without making friends. In fact, there is nobody who I would like to receive at my home when the domestic tradition is telling me to do this: to have teas and drinks, open the doors at any time for friends.*
>
> Tatiana, Russian,
> five years abroad (Germany, the Netherlands)

We already heard about Tatiana in Chapter 3: she suffered from depression and lived in a local village, unfortunately without much contact with locals. Like her, some internationals stay at home, hide from the host culture, and avoid being confronted with the external world. The Internet may fuel this marginalization by making it easy to develop feelings of connectedness with the expat's native country. It allows continued daily interactions with people from the home culture, whether by emails, virtual social networks (Facebook, Twitter), online forums, online chatting, or web surfing. This behaviour can become excessive and overwhelming; before the expat realizes it, virtual encounters are more frequent than physical encounters with people from their neighbourhood, and the lure of this virtual social life holds them back from going out and facing reality.

How much time a day do you spend on the virtual world of the Internet? Keep a log for a few days and, every day, record the time you spend on virtual relationships. You may be surprised.

We will see next that some studies suggest that positive feelings spread more easily (or only) between people who live within a short distance from each other.

How to Make Your Integration a Success

To summarize, expat life can be made easier by following these basic pieces of advice:

— Connect and make an effort to understand the local culture, the locals, and your surroundings. Nobody is forcing you to like it, but you need to understand it in order to find your way in this new place.

— Connect with international people who will provide you with emotional support, because they have been or still are confronted with similar issues and feelings as you. They will be able to provide you with "survival tips," help you find your way, and open your eyes to many other cultures.

— Stay connected with your own culture. You may see it with new eyes, and perhaps some of your convictions will be questioned and abandoned. You will also discover what makes you unique.

— Avoid intolerant groups and beware of co-national groups or isolated expats. Some groups are like cultural islands and look like a safe place away from the scary real world, but in fact many of their members might be quite intolerant and scoff at other cultures and at the host culture in particular. These groups are very destructive.

International Networks

Two researchers, Nicholas Christakis and James Fowler, found that some behaviours and health issues, such as obesity, losing weight, smoking, quitting smoking, happiness, and loneliness can all be "contagious." Loneliness, contagious? When I first read these results, I was intrigued. How can loneliness be contagious? Aren't lonely people too isolated to be contagious?

Christakis and Fowler argue that healthy behaviours, unhealthy behaviours, happiness, and loneliness are all transmissible by friends, friends of friends, and even their friends: people who do not know each other at all can transmit behaviours through invisible influences in social networks. This is not only because networks tend to share the same geographic areas or similar social environments; independently of the external similarities, people's values and behaviours can strongly influence those around them and spread to their friends' acquaintances whom they have never met. Friends' friends influence each other's behaviours without any of them being aware of it.

If networks have an important impact on loneliness, feelings of happiness, or health, this must concern us, because these circles obviously change drastically when we change country, depending on our adaptation style and external factors.

In the USA, on average 52% people in one's network know each other (given that the USA is quite an individual culture with high mobility, it is likely that these numbers are even higher in many regions of the world). Christakis and Fowler show that having strong connections within networks makes people healthier and happier. Independent of your income, education, gender, or age, you are 15% more likely to be happy if you are connected with one person who is happy; 10% more likely if a friend's friend is happy, and 6% more likely if a friend's friend's friend is happy.

It is a complex system because you have many friends of friends and so forth, and some are happy, some are not; they are all happy or unhappy to varying degrees. However, on average, taking all these varied dimensions into account and controlling for influencing factors, the scientific evidence suggests that a happy friend increases your chances of becoming happier more than an unhappy friend influences you to become unhappier. As a consequence, the more friends you have, the higher your chances of becoming happier.

Networks are high in transitivity when people of the network have many and strong connections: they know many of their friends' friends or their neighbour's neighbours. The network of a foreigner who has recently arrived in a new place is certainly not high in transitivity – quite the contrary. As a foreigner, you have few acquaintances and fewer opportunities to meet and connect with these acquaintances' friends, neighbours, colleagues, or family. Furthermore, internationals are at high risk of losing their international friends frequently due to geographic moves. Typically, expat networks are very fragile and low in transitivity compared to the networks of people who stay in the same location for many years.

As is commonly known in psychology, once you are conscious of the influence of a phenomenon on your behaviours, you have more freedom to act upon, avoid, or encourage this influence. In this case, while realizing the weakness of your networks, you can decide to change some of your habits to strengthen your social networks. There are several solutions.

First, you can directly influence how many friends and acquaintances you have ("friends" taken here in its broad sense as people with whom you feel comfortable). It is not straightforward – if it was all easy, you would probably not have opened this book in the first place.

Going to a party or entering a room with many people we do not know, and having to introduce ourselves and talk to strangers, is a situation that most of us dread. We know, objectively, there is no risk at all; however, it is often unpleasant at the start, and it is normal for this situation to generate some anxiety and fear. Fear or anxiety of meeting new people is something to learn to overcome when living an international life.

Most internationals interviewed have experienced these feelings and report that overcoming them and meeting a diversity of people is one of the things they enjoyed most and learned from the most when living a nomadic life.

There is no magic formula; you simply have to get out there and shake hands… but, as we discussed earlier, listen instead of trying to show others you are nice and smart. Remind yourself that most people in the room are also afraid of meeting new people. Just remain yourself, remain modest, and develop a compassionate attitude; cultivate a curiosity for others and show generosity towards them; and avoid the selfish attitude of worrying about what others think about you.

> — *The country does not matter; it is up to me to have good social network, so the place does not matter.*
> Dimitrova, Serbian,
> five years abroad (the USA, Spain)

> — *Find a person you can call. It is important to be around and be seen: in the neighbourhood, at school or at a local club. People will start to know you, and it will be easier to look for help if you need it. It is also the start of your new social network.*
> Cintia, Portuguese,
> eight years abroad (Brazil, the Netherlands, the United Arab Emirates, Singapore)

— Get out of the house. If you work, it is easier to meet people... But if you do not, it is the hardest. Go out and meet people. If you have kids, join kids clubs, international clubs, school clubs... to meet other people. Also good to find out how the system works... so ask people instead of spending a lot of time trying to find out how the system works by yourself.

Vanessa, French,
seventeen years abroad (Germany, England, Australia, Japan, the Netherlands)

— Be extremely open and do not reject any invitation for party/dinner/whatever. That's the only way to meet as many people as possible, which is the most important thing to do in a brand new place. By doing this, you will make your own circle of close friends after some time.

Tijana, Serbian,
two years abroad (the Netherlands, Hungary)

Another way to strengthen your network is to influence how densely connected it is. When you organize a regular coffee morning or a reading club, you create a much stronger network than if you know all the people individually but they have not met each other. Therefore, it is useful to seize opportunities to not only build links between yourself and your contacts but also to encourage your contacts to build links with each other, whether by organizing dinners, guided visits, or outings with friends.

The meetings have to be frequent or regular to enable strong social bonds to develop. Consider joining sport clubs; singing, dance, or meditation classes; or any activity that can be practised in a group, or organize your own book club or international diner once a month. Just send an email to neighbours, colleagues, and new acquaintances suggesting a monthly meeting in a pub or cafe, and see how it goes....

You may want to change your attitude during meetings as well. I enjoyed it recently when a friend invited me out and, instead of leaving me to find my way among her guests alone, she introduced me to the other people one after another and emphasized the things we had in common. This avoided the awkward situation of having nothing to say to each other aside from commenting on the weather. It is important to truly help your friends and contacts meet each other and, when possible, become acquainted with each other.

The turnover of friends is painful in international circles. After a few years, most of your friends have moved abroad and are far away from you. You can keep in touch by email and Internet easily, but this will not be enough. Christakis and Fowler shows that geographic proximity matters. When a friend who lives less than about one mile (1.6 km) away becomes happy, it can increase the probability that you are happy by 25%.

In contrast, the happiness of a friend who lives further away does not have a significant effect. The spread of happiness, as well as many other feelings, thoughts, values, or behaviours, seems to depend as much on face-to-face interactions as on deep personal connections. This emphasizes the need for the expat to engage in local life with other expats or with locals, as long as they live nearby.

> — *My best friends here were those who arrived at the same time as we did. They are all gone. Since then, I am more distant with people because I've suffered by getting attached to people who all have ended up leaving. I am exaggerating perhaps a little bit; I am making friends, but fewer though.*
>
> Christine, French, twelve years abroad (the Netherlands)

Christine (from the example above) told me that she can deal with having fewer friends because of her strong relationship with her husband, who is a strong support to her. If your friends are also foreigners, expats, or immigrants, the chances are very high that you, like Christine, will lose them sooner or later because they are more mobile than locals.

It is understandable then that you may feel like keeping a distance in your attachments, even if this means the relationships with new friends feel a little bit more superficial, more transitory. However, this is different from not making the effort to make new friends at all. Because of the high turnover of international people, the need to actively seek new acquaintances is even more important. As we have seen in previous parts of the book, to achieve this we need to develop more openness and appreciation for diversity (see Chapter 3 on loneliness, and Chapter 8 on building trust and friendship).

> *— I feel, in a situation of expatriation, people grow closer more quickly and friendships develop more quickly and sometimes more intensely than with friends in my home country who all have very busy lives too and with whom it is more difficult to find time to spend together.*
>
> Ike, lived thirteen years abroad as a child (Sweden, Ghana, the Netherlands, France, Mexico) and six as an adult (Cambodia, Thailand, Congo, Senegal)

PART 3

BALANCED LIFE

Chapter 10

Finding Strength, Meaning, and Balance

The human being is a living organism with its own developmental path written in its genes. However, for genes to be expressed properly and enable the individual to reach its best potential, the human body needs specific environmental conditions, just like seeds will turn into trees only if they get nutriments such as water, minerals, and sun. Obviously, we have physiological needs – like water, food or sleep – but less known is that we also have basic psychological needs that drive many of our behaviours. If the environment enables the basic psychological needs to be fulfilled, we blossom. If it doesn't, our psychological development and well-being is weakened.

In spite of having material comfort and even when travelling with a very loving partner, internationals might feel that something fundamental is missing from their new life. There is a confusing feeling of loss, or of not being one's self or of losing one's identity. Sometimes there is a sense of emptiness in spite of all the long to-do lists, and perhaps an inability to fill in the hours of solitude. We may be surprised to find ourselves suddenly wondering about the meaning of life. When this occurs, some basic psychological nutriments are probably missing.

Three Fundamental Psychological Needs

Edward Deci and Richard Ryan from the University of Rochester in the US have developed a theory of motivation, the self-determination theory. They uncovered three fundamental psychological needs, which they compare to the basic nutriments essential for our psychological growth, mental health, and well-being. These three basic needs are autonomy, competence, and connectedness. We need all three to be fulfilled and to blossom in life.

The need for autonomy is about having control of our choices, in particular those relating to our activities and goals in life. When we live in an over-controlling environment, we lose our freedom. In this condition, the need for autonomy is not fulfilled. This can lead to very painful experiences. For example, a child may enjoy playing the piano, but as she develops and is forced to take many piano lessons, she may start to hate the activity; every day her motivation becomes lower and external incentives will not work. Similarly, you may feel coerced into going to a place you don't like going to (for example, to work or to a party where you don't know anybody). If you don't feel free to choose to go, your need for autonomy and freedom of choice is affected, and, as a consequence, you lose motivation to continue. You feel the urge to decide for yourself and to be free to do so. When a need is not fulfilled, there is a craving for it. The psychological need becomes stronger.

The need for competence predicts that we need to feel we have an effect on our environment and that our activities are in harmony with our sense of self. We enjoy being challenged and discovering that we can achieve things with a fair amount of effort. When the environment is too boring or, on the contrary, when the task seems over-challenging, motivation is lost or becomes sub-optimal. "Too easy" is not worth it, and "too difficult" is discouraging. The psychological need for competence drives our desires to learn more and to further our personal growth, for example, by becoming a better person or deciding to register for evening classes to learn something new.

The need for connectedness or relatedness is our desire to feel connected to others, to love and care for others, and to be loved and cared for by others. We have a strong need for relationships, intimacy, and love, and for a sense of belonging to a community. When people reject or ignore us, we feel an intense pain. We start to be cognitively dysfunctional and withdrawn, and this has physiological consequences: in the long term, the immune system can become weakened (see Chapter 3 on loneliness).

After arriving in a new country, an expat's ability to fulfil the three fundamental psychological needs can become very difficult or be thwarted entirely, and for some this is a traumatic experience. They may feel that something fundamental is missing or have the sense they have lost something so important that a part of their identity is missing.

A common issue among most internationals – and one of their biggest complaints – is that there is little connectedness: people feel isolated and miss having friendships. The expert expats know what to do: get out and meet people as quickly as possible; do not be demanding or picky when selecting new friends; do not expect to find people "just like you"; and remain open and tolerant to new ways of thinking. We have seen these issues discussed in previous chapters.

For those who overcome their initial sense of isolation and learn new ways of associating with a wide range of very diverse persons, the environment will soon provide many opportunities to develop friendship. Actually, with time, people who have travelled abroad a lot learn to find each other and seek out the company of other internationals. A new sense of community develops based not on similar geographic roots or similar language and culture but on the similar life experience that comes from developing a strong taste for novelty and cultural diversity.

The second fundamental need, the need for autonomy, can also be extremely jeopardized in a new country. This is especially strong for a partner who follows the other without a strong conviction and who has accepted this life change for the sake of the other person instead of for personal reasons. It is easier to accept challenges when they are considered a part of our personal growth. By contrast, when faced with challenges that are not of our choosing, some people adopt a passive attitude and start to blame others for their situation. Instead of seeing the new life abroad as an opportunity to learn and develop, they feel forced by their family, partner, or employer to live "in a prison" and remain in a situation they hate. This is the start of a downward spiral, because the need for autonomy is seriously compromised. Resentment, hate, and regrets can be overwhelming and destructive and lead to chronic stress and perhaps depression and other health issues.

However, for many people, this same situation leads to the opposite feeling: many internationals are very happy to be free from their past life, perhaps because they are escaping from a former toxic relationship, a conformist and boring lifestyle, or an authoritarian and intrusive family. For them, this experience gives them a formidable sensation of freedom and independence. Their need for autonomy is totally fulfilled, and they will enjoy the freedom they now have to behave differently without the past constraints and to start following their chosen way, their own ideas. They feel that they can now fully blossom.

The third fundamental need, the need for competence, can be a difficult need for some people to meet while others may find it very easy to fulfil. We may arrive in a place where we speak neither the local language nor an alternative like English, and we may know nothing about the culture and find we are constantly making mistakes. The challenges may seem too great, so we become discouraged. The sense that there is too much to do and that we can never achieve what we want can be especially strong among the perfectionists. They may start to compare their present situation with their past situation where the environment was more predictable and provided a strong sense of control.

The reverse is usually true for people who feel energized by the discovery of new challenges. For people with a high desire to discover new things and who are very open to change, the environment provides many nutriments to feed their need for competence: for them, their situation is a unique opportunity to learn about many new things, whether it is architecture, natural life, new religions, languages, festivities, sports and games, technologies, rituals, social life, social behaviours, or social rules, etc. The opportunity for personal growth is enormous.

Identity and Sense of Cohesion

After a few months of living abroad without prior experience, a person's sense of identity might be impaired. There is a vague feeling that life is not meaningful anymore, and they may feel they lack direction or have the sense of going nowhere, being a nobody, and building nothing – just being there doing nothing valuable, nothing interesting, and nothing important! Do you recognize this type of feeling? These can all be linked to the fact that one or several of our three basic psychological needs have been thwarted by the situation. Newcomers may momentarily lose their sense of competence (their perceived ability to master skills and reach goals), their sense of autonomy (the freedom to choose and to live in harmony with their own values), and their sense of belonging (giving and receiving love and care).

As children, our sense of identity is given to us by our parents, our education, and our environment. If you are told you are lazy, courageous, or good at math, or that you have an attention disorder, you will internalize it. You think this is you, even if it's not true.

This still occurs in adulthood, although with time and experience, we have more and more freedom to think for ourselves and to discover what we are really like as we face various life situations. If life did not put us into challenging situations, the chances are that our identity would be more limited. Our sense of identity would come from a position at work, or from our family, for example. We would be more likely to be defined by other's expectations and be too busy to give it much thought.

However, when we are cut from our roots, we may feel lost in emptiness, and we certainly spend much more time alone. It may become harder to define what we should do and who we should be. This is a normal process to go through during a life transition.

We can turn this discomfort to our own advantage and see it as a wonderful opportunity and a privilege. Though it is a very uncomfortable position to be in, we can choose to see the new environment as a golden opportunity to reflect and re-assess our values and goals. Our time abroad can be a unique opportunity to prepare a diploma on-line, start a new job, invest time in a new hobby, or volunteer for a cause we care about – all without following the same path that was expected of us back home.

Bouncing Back after Difficult Life Events in Ten Steps

How do we cope with the loss and confusion created by important life changes and thrive after life-changing events? Solutions are found in the scientific literature on resilience. Resilience is an English word that means to become stronger and better at overcoming obstacles in the long-term. It involves the ability to cope well with high levels of ongoing disruptive change, to sustain good health and energy when under constant pressure, to bounce back easily after setbacks, to overcome adversity, to feel in harmony with the new environment, to feel in control of our environment and destiny, and to be at peace with our traumatic past.

Resilience comes from a positive adaptation to difficult past events. It means that something has been gained following the trauma. It does not mean that something lost has been recovered but that something else, an inner strength, has been built. It is the opposite of feeling like a victim, even in situations where we are objectively victims (such as in accidents or wars). It is a state of mind, and one that can definitely be learned and improved. It builds up over time, after obstacles and traumas have been thrown at us and we have learned (the hard way) to overcome, conquer, and find a new balance and well-being again. It is about learning to heal, in spite of the losses and the pain. It takes courage, and it takes time.

You can be broken down by adverse events in your life. You can get sick, depressed, or engage in dangerous behaviours to release your anger, or you can drink alcohol to help you forget. Instead of withdrawing into your own world, you can also choose to build stronger character by mastering your emotions and stress, overcoming the negative thoughts, focusing on the positive things in your life, and engaging in constructive behaviours.

The American Psychological Association (APA) suggests

ten ways to build resilience. Depending on life circumstance, personal factors, personality, former education, and culture, some people naturally develop certain of these skills rather than others. Most of them were described earlier and will sound familiar to you by now, while others will be newer.

The first way to develop resilience is to build and maintain supportive relationships. We have seen in previous chapters that social isolation is one of the main risk factors of living abroad and that you need to be socially active to build close relationships with the new people you encounter. This involves accepting help and support from others and, if possible, also providing love and care to others. Social support is absolutely critical to well-being and mental health in the long term (and, as we just saw, it has been defined as one of our three most fundamental psychological needs). It is also one of the strongest factors supporting the development of resilience.

The second important factor is to avoid seeing stressful events and life changes as unbearable problems. You can choose to react in positive ways to difficult events, even though some things are very painful and some things are definitely lost. You may feel you have lost your chance at a life goal or lost a career, for example, but if you avoid dwelling in the past or dwelling on losses, you can build resilience. Focus your attention on the things you have gained from the experience and ask yourself the following: What can be improved in the future? What did you learn from this experience that will be valuable for the future? What did you learn about yourself? What did you learn about other cultures? Did the entire experience help you in becoming more open, tolerant, and eager to learn new things, or perhaps better at building friendships? Did it improve your relationship, and, if not, what can be learned that could make your present and future relationships better and more meaningful?

Tan Phan studied how Vietnamese refugee women cope with being immigrants in Canada and found that they have developed a strong sense of meaning and purpose. They report that their suffering is worth it if their children succeed and achieve a better future in Canada. They also benefit from the strong support of their extended families and friends in Vietnamese ethno-cultural community.

> *— I was not happy with my career in Australia. This move forced me to walk away, which I was too scared to do, and I'm not sure if I ever would have. I do not think I would have known any different if I stayed in my home country all of my life. You make the most of what you have. The main positives from this experience would be personal growth. I have forced myself out of my comfort zone in Australia. I am learning a new language, studying at university (correspondence with an Australian university), seeing and living in a different culture.*
> Amy, Australian,
eight months abroad (France)

The third way to build resilience is to accept circumstances that cannot be changed. This part is difficult. Time helps, and so does compassion – in particular, compassion for oneself. Look around you and rediscover what you still have. Cultivate gratitude for the things you have and do not take them for granted. Writing down some of the things you are grateful for can help improve well-being when repeated several times over a couple of weeks. This exercise helps you to focus on the positive sides of your life and diminishes or removes regrets and anger following losses. Mindfulness training can also help you to learn to accept the present as it is, including pain and losses, without feeling overwhelmed.

The fourth way to build resilience is to develop realistic goals and move towards them. For example, make a list of dreams: the things you don't do because you do not have enough time or money. Also, think about the things you enjoyed doing in the past but stopped doing. Then select your top three and think about ways to realize these goals. Be as specific as possible. Often, we do not take the time to think about our dreams and so they remain very vague.

You can begin realising some of your dreams from the moment you start to make them actionable: for example, perhaps you dreamed about learning to scuba dive but never took any serious action towards that goal. Ask yourself when you want to try scuba diving: once on a future vacation, or every year, or perhaps once a week? Could you learn to scuba dive during a vacation or at the swimming pool at a local sports centre? Be specific. Then find out how much it costs and evaluate how much money you need to save and how long it would take to save this money.

After some thinking, preparation, gaining information, and taking action, many dreams are achievable within a period of just a few years. Moving towards dreams is in itself a drastic improvement for well-being and mental health. The journey matters as much as the destination.

The fifth recommendation for building strong resilience is to take decisive action in adverse situations. You cannot speak the local language? Learn it. You have a lot of administrative papers that need to be completed before you get a working permit? Make it a priority and take action to get it done. Do not procrastinate or avoid the issues; face them. Take breaks as well (see recommendation number ten, below) but work regularly and steadily towards solutions.

> *— Do one thing per day. When I arrived here in the Netherlands, I was so shocked that I had to force myself to go out. I did not want to talk to anyone (or anyone talk to me) because I was embarrassed that I did not know the language. Weird? Absolutely, but I was in a situation different to anything I'd ever encountered. So one thing a day, even if it is going to a museum by yourself, getting a cell phone, going shopping, etc. The only catch: try to do new things everyday. If you are shopping at one store, after a couple weeks, change it up. The more you jump in and get yourself out there, the better you will acclimatise.*
> Julia, Canadian,
two years abroad (England, the Netherlands)

The sixth recommendation is to look for opportunities for self-discovery. As we have seen in an earlier chapter, many internationals are aware and happy to have learned a lot from their international experience and have gained a lot of strength from it, as well as openness, tolerance, a better ability to deal with daily stresses, and knowledge. Take some time for yourself in the coming days and find a quiet place to reflect and think about your arrival in the new country. Feel the strengths gained from the experience and enjoy this feeling. It will make you feel good about yourself. If this exercise is difficult, try to make a list on paper of the things that are making it difficult for you to adapt, and then try to discover what this reveals about yourself: what does it tell you about your personality as compared to other people's? What do you like and dislike? How do you react to stress? What is your attitude towards building new relationships?

Trying to discover ourselves enables us to adapt our reactions: instead of reacting in an automatic way (our old-fashioned ways), we can observe our own reactions and choose to react in a new and more appropriate way. For example, we can feel irritated by a local custom but choose to react with patience. This gives us more freedom.

> — *Being an expat is not really ideal for me, but I try to make the most of it and discover novel aspects of my life here, e.g. travelling, concerts, museums, and other activities that I wouldn't be able to do in my home country/town. [...] I think that living away from my country has been an important element in developing my personality and character, making me more open-minded and flexible, and increasing my awareness and consideration for people characters and cultures. Also, I had the chance to experience a variety of situations, engage in various activities, travel, and make friends. [...] I'm not particularly happy here. I do try.*
>
> Kelly, Greek,
> two years abroad (the UK, the Netherlands)

The seventh observation made about people who have a strong resilience is that they nurture a positive view about themselves. Developing confidence in your abilities to solve your problems is very important for building resilience. Self-confidence can be seriously jeopardized after a move abroad because we have to learn new ways of solving issues, especially when dealing with people who have different values and attitudes. It is important not to blame ourselves when we fail to get something done. It is truly difficult at the start and takes time to get settled, as testimonies in this book have shown. Do not procrastinate and spiral downwards when you encounter things that are unknown to you. Use the ABCDE technique (see the Appendix) or the relaxation and visualisation techniques from Chapter 4 to develop calmness and self-compassion. Accept and love yourself – not in a selfish and narcissistic way but by simply and objectively accepting your own limits.

The eighth recommendation is to keep things in perspective. Try to consider the stressful situation in a broader context. There are different strategies you can use, depending on your preferences. One woman told me that she visualised the Earth as if she was seeing it from the perspective of an astronaut; it helped her see how small her problems were compared to the size of our entire world. Contemplating the stars at night gives me the nice feeling of belonging to something much bigger than my personal problems.

Listening to, seeing or reading about other people's issues can also help bring our own worries into perspective. Life abroad brings us closer to new forms of human suffering and new types of poverty, discrimination, diseases, or security issues. For example, some international workers witness the consequences of other countries' hunger, violence, epidemics, natural disasters or wars. Expats who have witnessed other's suffering tend to see their own issues as less important than they did before.

The ninth recommendation for building resilience is to maintain an optimistic outlook, as we discussed in the first part of the book. This involves focusing on what we want to achieve rather than allowing ourselves to be invaded by negative thoughts or driven by fears and worries. The best way to cope with issues is to plan and take action while thinking about what we will get from the experience rather than about what we have lost. Seligman, a specialist in resilience and optimism, recommends the use of Ellis' methods (the ABCDE technique) to build an optimistic mindset.

The tenth way to build resilience, according to the APA, is to take care of ourselves. We need to put our health (physical health and psychological health) first on our list of priorities. This includes exercising regularly to keep a strong body and a good immune system, and maintaining a healthy lifestyle, including good sleeping habits, a good diet, warm and meaningful relationships with people we love, and regular health check-ups.

We also need to take care of our emotional balance and take the time to engage in activities that are relaxing and pleasant. We can keep in mind the 1:3 ratio of negativity-positivity discovered by Frederickson (cf. Chapter 5) and make an attempt to add positive moments in our daily lives. This works for building resilience as well.

Building a stronger resilience and learning to better cope with life events and difficult moments does not mean that facing difficulties is less painful. Resilient people probably experience the same pain as less-resilient people. However, having a resilient mind-set helps diminish the destructive impact of difficult life events. It prevents the resilient person from spiralling downwards into victim mode and enables them to keep moving toward their goals, enjoy the good aspects of their life, and build further plans optimistically.

Chapter 11

Enjoying Life Abroad

Personally, I believe I am happier and more creative than I would have been had I chosen a traditional life and career in my own country. I know I have lost opportunities – I am not a professor in a French university and I do not have a nice house in Champagne near my family – but I am pleased that I dared to follow another road than the one that was expected of me by my family, my former teachers, and my culture in general. The road I took is based on my deepest values, and the extraordinary diversity of people I have met by experiencing life abroad and meeting people in international communities is something I would never have found had I stayed in my own country. The learning curve has been dramatic, from new places and new people to new jobs and new hobbies.

Most internationals I interviewed during the preparation of this book shared similar feelings. The experience of living in a foreign country made them more creative, more daring, and less fearful of the unknown. They became more resilient, feeling both stronger in the face of problems and better able to put things into perspective and not worry about small issues. They also developed better abilities to connect with men and women from other backgrounds and cultures. They report having learned a lot from others and also from themselves.

The majority of the expats and internationals I interviewed told me that they definitely do not regret their choice to move to a new country, in spite of the obstacles they encountered, and few wished to return to their home countries.

Millions of expats and internationals live abroad and enjoy the experience and its challenges. They feel special because they know they have grown stronger and more open, developed the ability to see issues from different perspectives, and become more resilient to life changes. I thought that giving them a voice was a fair way to conclude this book, and I hope their examples will inspire you.

> — *When I was a teenager, I used to be very insecure with low self-esteem. Through my travelling experiences (seeing yourself through other people's eyes), I realised I was kinda alright. Also I was thrown into the deep end quite often since I travelled alone most of the time, so you learn that every beginning is difficult but that there is always a light at the end of the tunnel; you just need to be patient. I learnt I was actually good at certain things, and I made friendships that will last forever, which made me a richer and stronger person.*
> Edda, Dutch,
> nine years abroad (Israel, England, Scotland, Mexico, Turkey, Greece)

> — *Living as an expat, you learn to be respectful of people from all walks of life. [...] I work and socialise with a wider range of people than perhaps I would have otherwise done. [...] I am less easily shocked by different behaviours and lifestyles. [...] I have learnt that there are many positive aspects of different cultures, and that by experiencing them first-hand you break down your own prejudices and see things differently from "the inside."*
> Richard, British,
> fourteen years abroad (the Netherlands)

— *Expatriation leads to more open-mindedness and more understanding. It does not mean you have to like what you see but you have to be aware of it. Like, the Dutch people are not flexible and think that their way is the best. If you disagree, it does not matter; you just have to understand that culturally, they are like that... accept it, embrace it, without liking it. Once you know how to do that, you are very flexible! [...] I learned about my own culture and found out after a few years that it is not as perfect as it appeared to me originally. [...] Living in different countries, meeting different people, you also start losing all the stereotypes you have about different people... including yourself: Dutch people are stingy, French people are arrogant, US citizens think their country is the best... but individually people are just people. [...] When you meet people who have experienced different things (like wars, refugees...) you see your own life differently.*

Vanessa, French,
seventeen years abroad (Germany, Australia, Japan,
the Netherlands, UK)

— *My new strengths? Cultural awareness and understanding; open minded, flexible, adaptable, can-do attitude; questioning and building on others rather than criticising and complaining; respect for others and their culture and beliefs (there's no right or wrong, just different perspectives); [...] having learned to ask WHY first, hold judgement, be curious to learn more; having learned to consciously try new things that feel uncomfortable but are "normal" for other cultures, like eating with your hands or going into the sauna all naked with people from both sexes.*

Cintia, Portuguese,
eight years abroad (Brazil, the Netherlands,
the United Arab Emirates, Singapore)

— *What I've learned from living abroad? Flexibility, putting things into perspective, being patient.*

Myntje, Dutch,
one year abroad (South Africa)

— *I think it is a great opportunity to travel and live abroad for anyone. It is a great process for making new friends, learning new things, and also it is psychologically very fruitful for one's personality. [...] It is important to learn new cultures and meet people; it expands your mind and makes people less self-centred and embedded in their own way of thinking and understanding life.*

Tijana, Serbian,
two years abroad (the Netherlands, Hungary)

— *I feel like I am more sensitive to cultural differences now than I used to be. Having lived in Buddhist and Muslim societies, I feel like I know their religious customs and traditions better and I am better able to understand and respect them. I have learned to be more flexible, as I have had to adapt to new ways of life and cultures, which also allows me to put my own background and practices into perspective.*

Ike, lived thirteen years abroad as a child
(Sweden, Ghana, the Netherlands, France, Mexico)
and six as an adult (Cambodia, Thailand, Congo, Senegal)

— *I am more calm, more independent. I know I can do it. [...] Expatriation is a unique opportunity to meet other people, and it is great. Especially when you move out of Europe, it is really a different life. (...) No, I do not want to go back in Europe (Paris, London or Brussels). And I wish we will have the opportunity to move again for a new experience.*

Marie, Belgium,
four years abroad (Sao Paulo, Brazil)

I hope the book has built a bridge between the insights of psychology and neuroscience, and shown how these insight can be applied to increase the well-being and daily life of an expat. Psychology can make a huge difference in people's lives, and I believe this now more than ever before because of what happened after this manuscript was finished....

EPILOGUE

While writing the last two chapters of this book, a new chapter in my life began: I learned that I had ovarian cancer.

I will not recount here this new road race, as it is not the focus of this book. However, my experience does serve as an illustration of how helpful psychological knowledge can be for overcoming life traumas and changes, such as moving abroad, changing jobs, getting sick, or going through other important life transitions and losses. So let me tell you, as a conclusion, what helped me the most out of all the tips and knowledge I have shared in the book.

First, these last months have reminded me that it is important to develop good mental habits and practice them every day, perhaps especially when there are no main issues in your present life.

At the time my cancer was diagnosed, I was divorced and a single mother working as a scientist in a multinational company. I could have complained that I was alone in a foreign country without my family, but the fact is that I had never felt better. Writing the book had helped me to overcome my fear of loneliness and motivated me to work less hours, practise more sports, and start discovering meditation. I felt lucky, given the circumstances, that the disease had been discovered at a moment in my life when I felt very happy, resilient, and independent. It did not prevent me from experiencing lots of pain and anxiety, but it did help me to cope better.

Mental balance is not something that we reach one day and keep for the rest of our lives. We change, and our environment changes. Traumas or daily stresses can accumulate over time in this constantly shifting environment. This is why we benefit from daily "maintenance" at the psychological level: the practice of ABCDE exercises and relaxation exercises, the building of new social networks and new friendships, the practice of sports, the development of meditation techniques and writing....

Each one of us will make choices that work for our own situation and personality. However, whatever choices we make, it is important to keep taking care of our body and mind on a daily basis (see my book recommendations on stress management and happiness in the next pages). When difficult times come again, and they always will, having these mental habits will give you the strength to stand the pain, get through it, and stand up again after having fallen.

During my treatment, I was also reminded of how difficult it is to accept help. When people learned about my illness, the amount of help and support I received surpassed all my expectations. I was surrounded by love and warmth by my friends, my colleagues, my family abroad, my ex-in-laws, people from my rowing team, the parents and teachers from the international school where my son was, and even some anonymous readers (I had just started the expatscience.com blog a few months earlier). It was so much that it felt embarrassing! But receiving this help and accepting it helped me carry on with my difficult treatments and with my life.

I progressively understood that I was now part of a new community: the cancer survivors. It was reassuring to meet people who had experienced similar life events. We shared our feelings and our tips on various ways to cope. Just as I once built my own network of friends and community after arriving in the Netherlands ten years ago, I've started to build another network of friends and contacts to sustain me, this time among cancer survivors. We are never alone.

There are many other things I have learned from facing cancer, just as there has been from living abroad. I will conclude by mentioning perhaps the most difficult challenge in both cases: for me, it was the feeling of not being in control – in other words, the feeling of losing my freedom and independence.

With cancer, I faced a death threat, and only surgeons and oncologists could save me. Was there anything I could do to help in my own healing process? I knew that feeling passive, as if you are a spectator of your own life, is very depressing, so I had to find out my own way to fight back and avoid helplessness. This new turn in my life led me to discover my new limits and my remaining strengths, and to use them to remain mentally healthy and physically active. My own path was to try to learn as much as possible about my cancer and about what patients can do to boost their immune systems, and to apply my new findings in my daily life. I became more hopeful, because I was trying to help my body to stay alive during treatments and then to heal.

What I learned from these experiences and drastic life changes was that staying in control does not mean we can go backward in life or control our destiny. For example, often we will not be able to go back to our home country, former home, or former job. Staying in control simply means that in spite of the unexpected losses and disappointments in life, we use the strength that remains to find new ways of achieving balance, meaning, and happiness. We have to extract the positive from life events and use it in our favour. It is not about achieving old dreams but about focusing on new solutions and adapting to the new circumstances.

When moving abroad, the most important gains from the overall experience are finding and meeting new people, and feeling part of new cultures (the host culture and the international culture). Use these insights in your favour. You may feel lost and helpless at the start, but you are in a process of building new strengths and new competencies. You are turning international.

REFERENCES

Chapter 2. The Arrival

Berry, J. W. (2006). Contexts of acculturation. In D. L. Sam & J. W. Berry (Eds.), *The Cambridge Handbook of Acculturation Psychology* (pp 27-42). Cambridge: Cambridge University Press.

Berry, J. W. (2006). Stress perspectives on acculturation. In D. L. Sam & J. W. Berry (Eds.), *The Cambridge Handbook of Acculturation Psychology* (pp 43-57). Cambridge: Cambridge University Press.

Ellis, A. & Harper, R. J. (1997). *A Guide to Rational Living*. North Hollywood: Wilshire Book Co. Third Edition.

Frederickson, B. L. (2009). *Positivity: Top-Notch Research Reveals the 3-to-1 Ratio That Will Change Your Life*. New York: Three Rivers Press.

Karren, K. J., Smith, N. L., Hafen, B. Q. & Jenkins, K. J. (2010). *Mind Body Health: The Effects of Attitudes, Emotions, and Relationships*. London: Benjamin Cummings.

Kosic, A. (2006). Personality and individual factors in acculturation. In D. L. Sam & J. W. Berry (Eds.), *The*

Cambridge Handbook of Acculturation Psychology (pp 113-128). Cambridge: Cambridge University Press.

Lyubomirksy, S. (2007). *The How of Happiness: A New Approach to Getting the Life You Want.* London: Penguin Books.

Masgoret, A. M. & Ward, C. (2006). Culture learning approach to acculturation. In D. L. Sam & J. W. Berry (Eds.), *The Cambridge Handbook of Acculturation Psychology* (pp 58-77). Cambridge: Cambridge University Press.

Ramirez, G. & Beilock, S. L. (2011). Writing about testing worries boosts exam performance in the classroom. *Science*, 14, 331, pp 211-213.

Seligman, M. E. P. (2006). *Learned Optimism, How to Change Your Mind and Your Life.* New York: Vintage Books, Random House.

Sternberg, E. M. (2001). *The Balance Within, the Science Connecting Health and Emotions.* New York: W. H. Freeman and Company.

Ward, C., Bochner, S. & Furnham, A. (2001). *The Psychology of Culture Shock.* Routledge, Taylor and Francis group, London. Second Edition.

Chapter 3. Loneliness

Cacioppo, J. T. & Patrick, W. (2008). *Loneliness: Human Nature and the Need for Social Connection.* London: W. W. Norton & Co.

Damasio, A. (2000). *The Feeling of What Happens.* London, Vintage Books.

Karren, K. J., Smith, N. L., Hafen, B. Q. & Jenkins, K. J. (2010). *Mind Body Health: The Effects of Attitudes, Emotions, and Relationships.* London: Benjamin Cummings.

Reis, H. T. (2001). Relationship experiences and emotional well-being. In C. D. Ryff & B. H., *Singer, Emotion, Social*

Relationships, and Health (pp. 57-86). New York: Oxford University Press.

Chapter 4. Acculturation Stress and Chronic Stress

Cornell, A. W. (1996). *The Power of Focusing: A Practical Guide to Emotional Self-Healing*. Oakland, Canada: Raincoast Books.

Davis, M., Eschelman, E. R., & McKay, M. (2008). *The Relaxation & Stress Reduction Workbook*. Oakland, Canada: Raincoast Books. Sixth Edition.

Karren, K. J., Smith, N. L., Hafen, B. Q. & Jenkins, K. J. (2010). *Mind Body Health, the Effects of Attitudes, Emotions, and Relationships*. London: Benjamin Cummings.

Mutrie, N. & Faulkner, G. (2004). Physical Activity: Positive Psychology in Motion. In P. A. Linley & S. Joseph, *Positive Psychology in Practice*. Hoboken, NJ: John Wiley & Sons.

Sapolsky, R. M. (2004). *Why Zebras Don't Get Ulcers: The Acclaimed Guide to Stress, Stress-Related Diseases, and Coping*. New York: Henry Holt and Company. Third Edition.

Ward, C., Bochner, S., & Furnham, A. (2001). *The Psychology of Culture Shock*. Routledge, Taylor and Francis group, London. Second Edition.

Chapter 5. Home Abroad

Bloom, P. (2010). *How Pleasure Works*. New York: W. W. Norton & Co.

Frederickson, B. L. (2009). *Positivity: Top-Notch Research Reveals the 3-to-1 Ratio That Will Change Your Life*. New York: Three Rivers Press.

Gilbert, D. T. (2006). *Stumbling on Happiness*. New York:

Knopf.

Hailey A., Helerman, Britt, T. W., & Hashima, P. Y. (2008). Ibasho and the adjustment, satisfaction, and well-being of expatriate spouses. *International Journal of Intercultural Relations, 32*, 282-299.

LeDoux, J. (1998). *The Emotional Brain: The Mysterious Underpinnings of Emotional Life*. Phoenix, London.

Siegel, D. J. (2007). *The Mindful Brain: Reflection and Attunement in the Cultivation of Well-Being*. New York: W. W. Norton and Co.

Sternberg, E. M. (2009). *Healing Spaces: The Science of Place and Well-Being*. London, The Belknap Press of Harvard University Press.

Chapter 6. Cultural Differences in Values and Attitudes

Hofstede, G. (2001). *Culture's Consequences: Comparing Values, Behaviors, Institutions, and Organizations across Nations*. London: Sage Publications.

Hofstede, G., Hofstede, G. J. & Minkov, M. (2010). *Cultures and Organizations: Software of the Mind*. McGraw-Hill, London.

Nisbett, R. E. (2003). *The Geography of Thought: How Asians and Westerners Think Differently... And Why*. London, Free Press.

Masuda, T. & Nisbett, R. E. (2001). Attending holistically vs. analytically: Comparing the context sensitivity of Japanese and Americans. *Journal of Personality and Social Psychology, 81*, 922-934.

Yarbus, A. (1967). *Eye Movements and Vision*. New York, Plenum Press.

Chapter 7. New Language and New Interactions

Ellis, R. (1997). *Second Language Acquisition*. New York, Oxford University Press.

Neville, H. J. (2005). Development and plasticity of human cognition. In U. Mayr, E. Awh & S. Keele (Eds.). *Developing Individuality in the Human Brain: A Tribute to Mike Posner*. Washington DC:APA Books, pp. 209-235.

Robson, D. (2011). Memory sticks: Do mnemonics work? *New Scientist*, 2806.

Ward, C., Bochner, S., & Furnham, A. (2001). *The Psychology of Culture Shock*. Routledge, Taylor and Francis group, London. Second Edition.

Chapter 8. From Strangers to Friends

Heider, F. (1958). *The Psychology of Interpersonal Relations*. New York: John Wiley & Sons.

Jones, E. E., Kanhouse, D. E., Kelley, H. H., Nisbett, R. E., Valins, S., & Weiner, B. (1972). *Attribution: Perceiving the Causes of Behavior*. New York: General Learning Press.

Karren, K. J., Smith, N. L., Hafen, B. Q., & Jenkins, K. J. (2010). *Mind/Body Health, the Effects of Attitudes, Emotions and Relationships*. London: Benjamin Cummings. Fourth Edition.

Kidder, T. (2009). *Strength in What Remains, a Journey of Remembrance and Forgiveness*. New York: Random House.

Reis, H. T. (2001). Relationship experiences and emotional well-being. In C. D. Ryff & B. H. Singer (Eds), *Emotion, Social Relationships, and Health*. New York: Oxford University Press, pp. 57- 86.

Chapter 9. Integration and Support Networks

Berry, J. W. (2006). Contexts of acculturation. In D. S. Sam & J. W. Berry, *The Cambridge Handbook of Acculturation Psychology*, Cambridge: Cambridge University Press, pp. 27-42.

Christakis, N. A., & Fowler. J. H. (2009). *Connected, the Surprising Power of Our Social Networks and How They Shape Our Lives*. New York: Little, Brown and Company.

Narayan, D. Patel, R. Schafft, K. Rademacher, A. & Koch-Schulte, S. (1999). *Voices of the Poor, Volume 1, Can Anyone Hear Us? Voices from 47 Countries*. New York, Oxford University Press.

Chapter 10. Finding Strength, Meaning and Balance

American Psychological Association. The Road to Resilience. Available on the APA Psychology Help Center's website: http://www.apa.org/helpcenter/road-resilience.aspx

Deci E. L. & Flaste, R. (1996). *Why We Do What We Do: Understanding Self-Motivation*. London: Penguin (Non-Classics).

Phan, T. (2006). Resilience as a coping mechanism: A common story of Vietnamese refugee women. In Paul T. P. Wong & Lilian C. J. Wong (Eds.), *Handbook of Multicultural Perspectives on Stress and Coping*. USA: Springer, USA, pp.427-438.

Ryan, R. M., & Deci, E. L. (2000). Self-determination theory and the facilitation of intrinsic motivation, social development, and well-being. *American Psychologist*, 55, 68-78.

Chapter 11. Enjoying Life Abroad

Oudenhoven, J. P. van (2006). Immigrants. In D. S. Sam & J. W. Berry, *The Cambridge Handbook of Acculturation Psychology*. Cambridge: Cambridge University Press, pp 163-180.

RESOURCES

A short list of books and websites I found accessible and useful:

Books

- *The Expert Expat* by Melissa Brayer Hess and Patricia Linderman (Nicholas Brealey, 2007) is packed with practical information to make your move abroad more efficient.

- *Raising Global Nomads* by journalist Robin Pascoe (*Expatriate Press*, Vancouver) is an entertaining and insightful guide to travelling with children.

- *The Miracle of Mindfulness* (Random House, 1975) written by the Vietnamese Buddhist monk Thich Nhat Nanh teaches us how to fully live in the present moment and enjoy what we already have without worrying about the past or the future.

- *Full Catastrophe Living* (Delacorte Press, 1990) by Jon J. Kabat-Zinn proposes a step-by-step program to learning meditation and relaxation; his method has been used internationally in stress-reduction programs.

- *A Woman in Your Own Right* (Quartet Books, 1982) by Anne Dickson discusses how to develop assertiveness,

be free of despair and anger and get what we want.
- On happiness and well-being, I especially enjoyed three books.
  - From Daniel Nettle, *Happiness: The Science behind Your Smile* (Oxford University Press, 2005) is an excellent introduction to this complex subject.
  - *Stumbling on Happiness* (Knopf, 2006) from Daniel Gilbert is very insightful and explains how to avoid some common pitfalls.
  - Sonja Lyobomirsky, in *The How of Happiness: A New Approach to Getting the Life You Want*, presents several methods that have been tested experimentally; it's a self-help book designed so that you can pick and choose the activities you prefer.

Websites

- Psychological help centre and information from the American Psychological Association: http://www.apa.org/helpcenter/
- Information on physical and mental health from the USA National Institute of Health: http://health.nih.gov/
- Suicide lines: List of help line per country from the International Association for Suicide prevention: http://www.iasp.info/resources/Crisis_Centres/
- Help for women in abusive relationships:
  - in the USA, http://www.866uswomen.org/Default.aspx
  - in Europe, Women against Violence Europe (Wave) http://www.wave-network.org/
  - in Europe, the USA and other countries, http://

www.hotpeachpages.net/a/countries.html

- For parents:
    - Third Culture Kids forum: www.tckkids.com
    - Foreign Service Youth Foundation: www.fsyf.org
    - Families in Global Transition: http://www.figt.org/ and http://www.incengine.org
- For non-native English speakers, idiomatic expressions: http://www.usingenglish.com/reference/idioms/

APPENDIX

ABCDE technique

A. Adversity: Write down a problem you are facing, and describe what you find really annoying, painful, frustrating about this situation.

B. Belief: What do you think your negative beliefs about this problem are? What is your interpretation of the situation? What negative gneralizations does this problem generate or support?

C. Consequence: Describe how you are feeling and how you are acting as a consequence of this belief.

D. Dispute: Think about other possible interpretations.In particular, imagine the point of view of the other persons, and the cultural differences.

E. Energize: Consider more optimistic explanations for your problem so that it energizes you, lifts your spirit, and so you become more hopeful, less anxious. Then take appropriate action. If it does not work at first, try again in a different way.

INDEX

A

ABCDE Technique 34-6, 40, 53, 66, 71, 72, 156, 199, 200, 207, 223
Abusive 82, 219
Acculturation 3, 17, 24, 55, 163, 164, 166-8, 170
Adaptation 18, 21, 25, 38, 56, 84, 90, 91, 93, 123, 125, 126, 163-5, 167, 171, 174, 175, 180, 194
Addiction 4, 81, 167
Alcohol, Alcoholism 28, 194
Alienation 28, 176
Ambiguity 18, 116
American Psychological Association 194
Anger 14, 34, 49, 59, 85, 139, 194, 196
Anxiety 12, 25, 28, 30, 40, 46, 49, 54, 61, 66, 67, 70, 71, 73, 75, 81, 116-8, 155, 167, 182, 207
Arrival 3, 10, 12, 16, 19-25, 59, 65, 73, 88, 127, 133, 165, 168, 177, 198
Asians 97, 98, 140
Assimilation 163, 165, 170
Attachment 45, 48, 49, 132
Attribution error 153
Authority 101, 105
Autonomic nervous system 50
Autonomy 49, 102, 110, 160, 189, 191, 192

B

Balance, balanced 3, 9, 12, 13, 27, 46, 48, 55, 63, 71, 158, 188, 194, 200, 207, 208
Belonging (sense of) 148, 158, 159, 176, 190, 193, 199
Berry, John 17, 163, 164, 166, 167, 173, 175
Blame 13, 18, 40, 153, 154, 191, 199
Block, John 30
Blood pressure 28, 30, 50, 63
Body language 141
Burnout 58, 59

C

Cacioppo, John 48
Cancer 43, 206-208
Cannon, Walter 55
Career 11, 27, 34, 38, 112, 127, 195, 196, 201
Christakis, Nicholas 180, 184
Cognitive appraisal 29, 30
Cognitive bias 153, 156
Cognitive techniques 34
Cognitive therapy(ies) 14, 34, 70
Collectivism, collectivist 109, 110, 112
Communication 91, 123, 125, 139, 140, 142, 151, 157
Compassion 41, 84, 85, 158, 196, 199
Competence 128, 160, 189, 190-2
Co-national(s) 171, 173, 176, 179
Confidence, self-confidence 11, 12, 28, 32, 40, 49, 85, 124, 157, 159, 172, 199
Conforming behaviours 18
Connectedness 51, 145, 149, 178, 189, 190
Conscious, consciously 50, 63, 79, 141, 168, 169, 181, 203
Consciousness 50, 143
Contagious 175, 180
Control 12, 17, 27, 28, 31-3, 40, 51, 56, 66, 87, 95, 144, 159, 189, 192, 194, 208
Convention(s) 109, 140, 141, 142
Conversation(s) 24, 73, 76, 85, 92, 116, 126, 129, 148, 155, 158
Coppola, Sophia 127

Cornell, Ann Weiser 69
Cortisol 57-9
Courage 66, 74, 194
Courtesy 18
Creative, creatively, creativity 18, 34, 40, 42, 48, 65, 84, 86, 87, 102, 155, 172, 201
Critical period 137
Cross-cultural 12, 14, 17, 91, 92, 99, 100, 123-5, 145
Cultural distance 17
Culture shock 10, 27, 31, 91, 107, 117, 168

D

Dale, Henry 45
Daring 201
Deafness, deaf 126, 127, 233
Deci, Edward 189
Deep breathing 61, 62, 64, 67
Depressed, depression 4, 12, 22, 24-6, 28, 31, 33, 35, 40, 49, 56, 58, 61, 72, 83, 84, 116, 146, 159, 167, 178, 191, 194
Diary 41
Disappointment(s) 25, 85, 208
Discourage(d) 13, 135, 177, 192
Discrimination 34, 170, 199
Diversity 17, 77, 86, 99, 114, 150, 182, 185, 191, 201
Divorce 32, 33, 44, 58

E

Ellis, Albert 34-6, 200
Emotion Regulation 55
Empathy 144, 149, 158, 159
Employee(s) 99, 101, 107, 112, 141, 155
Emptiness 44, 189, 193
Entrepreneurs, entrepreneurial 18, 117
Equality 17, 101
Ethnic group, ethnic community 165, 167, 168, 173, 174
Exhaustion 12, 58, 59, 83
Expat compounds 175
Expectations 8, 20, 38-40, 53, 85, 92, 93, 95, 99, 137, 173, 193, 207
Extraversion 159
Eye movements 94, 95

F

Facial expressions 116, 141
Fear(s) 40, 43, 44, 49, 53, 54, 66, 69, 70, 75, 85, 117, 150, 155, 176, 178, 182, 200, 206
Femininity 113-115
Flexibility 18, 33, 35, 123, 138, 139, 154, 155, 172, 203
Focus technique 51, 54, 66, 67, 70-72
Foreign accent 137
Fowler, James 180, 184
Frederickson, Barbara 30, 86, 87, 149, 200

Freedom 10, 17, 35, 82, 83, 87, 92, 101, 102, 105, 106, 119, 123, 159, 181, 189, 191-193, 198, 208
Frontal areas 50
Fulfilment, fulfilled 52, 87, 88, 147, 188, 189, 191
Future orientation 119

G

Gaze 141
Genes, genetic 43, 48, 188
Gestures 92, 116, 137, 142
Gottman, John 85
Gratitude 86, 87, 149, 196
Guilt, guilty 36, 85, 109

H

Happiness, happy, happier 11-13, 32, 52, 56, 59, 79, 87, 102, 116, 117, 145, 147, 159, 180, 181, 184, 191, 196, 198, 201, 207, 208
Harper, J. 36
Heart disease 28, 56
Heart rate 30, 50, 54, 57, 60, 66
Helping others 60, 87, 159, 160
Helpless, helplessness 10, 12, 27, 28, 29, 34, 85, 86, 123, 167, 208, 209
Hobby(ies) 47, 48, 128, 193, 201

Hofstede, Geert 99-101, 103, 108-110, 113, 115, 118, 120
Hofstede, Gert Jan 103, 110, 115, 118, 120
Homesickness, homesick 23, 24, 79, 81, 171
Homophily 149
Homosexuality 113, 114
Humiliation 109, 160
Hypocrisy, hypocritical 109, 141
Hypothalamus 57

I

Ibasho 74-77
Identity 17, 27, 28, 88, 146, 165, 170, 172, 189, 190, 192, 193
Immune system 32, 56, 57, 59, 63, 146, 190, 200, 208
Individualism, individualistic 109, 110, 112, 154
Indo-European language 134
Integration 3, 146, 160, 162, 163, 165, 167-170, 176, 179
International management 99
Internet 19, 166, 178, 179, 184
Intimacy 43, 85, 157, 158, 190
Intonation 138, 140
Invisible support 147, 148
Isolation 14, 32, 33, 43, 44, 46-48, 53, 59, 110, 112, 127, 146, 163, 171, 190, 195

J

Job(s) 10, 20, 24, 27, 28, 50, 58, 100, 101, 126, 127, 132-4, 160, 175, 193, 201, 206, 208
Joke(s) 155, 156

K

Kidder, Tracy 160
Kremen, Adam 30

L

Language classes 10, 128, 134, 139
Language(s) 3, 9, 10, 14, 20, 21, 24, 25, 34, 47, 73-75, 96, 112, 124-141, 147, 148, 156, 165, 166, 171-4, 176, 191, 192, 196, 197
Laugh 26, 73, 142, 151, 155, 156, 177
Ledoux, Joseph 49
Level of functioning 22, 23, 27
Linguistic 134, 162, 174
Linley, Alex 87
Loneliness, lonely 3, 32, 34, 36, 42-54, 59, 66, 68, 71, 81, 85, 112, 156, 180, 185, 190, 206
Long-term orientation 119, 120
Losada, Marcial 86
Loss 12, 28, 44, 46, 58, 139, 151, 172, 188, 194-6, 206, 208

Love 20, 43, 44, 77, 78, 85-7, 109, 142, 150, 151, 190, 193, 195, 199, 200, 207
Lyubomirsky, Sonia 87

M

Management, manager(s) 17, 99-101, 106, 107, 113
Marginalization 163, 165, 177, 178
Masculinity 113-5
Meaningful, Meaningfulness (of life) 146, 159, 192
Meditation 51, 65, 66, 72, 183, 207
Memories 39, 67, 70, 76-9, 127
Mindfulness 51, 66, 67, 196
Minkov, Michael 103, 110, 115, 118, 120
Mirror neurons 143, 144
Misunderstandings 126, 139, 142, 144, 151
Money 9, 10, 19, 31, 114, 116, 117, 120, 122, 127, 130, 149, 150, 159, 196, 197
Motivation(s) 40, 125, 128, 129, 132, 133, 171, 189, 190

N

Narayan, Deepa 176
Network(s) 14, 50, 51, 53, 79, 145, 146, 149, 162, 163,

165-8, 171, 175, 177, 178, 180-3, 207, 208
New language 124
Nisbett, Richard 96, 98, 99, 102
Nobel Prizes 102

O

Openness 41, 119, 123, 125, 168, 185, 198
Optimism, optimistic 11, 28, 34, 37, 38-40, 199, 200
Oxytocin 45

P

Pain 8, 43, 44, 49, 51, 61, 67, 70-2, 81, 84, 87, 150, 151, 156, 190, 194, 196, 200, 207
Parasympathetic system 57, 63
Personality 13, 18, 24, 29, 72, 81, 87, 150, 195, 198, 204, 207
Perspective(s) 14, 34, 35, 93, 106, 169, 199, 202-4
Pessimism, pessimistic 38, 40, 85
Phan, Tan 195
Phonemes 135, 136, 138
Physical activity 59, 72, 139
Politeness 109
Positive psychology 38, 86, 87
Positivity 86, 87, 200
Poverty 2, 176, 199
Power Distance 101-6
Proto-language 134-6

Psychological needs 44, 159, 188-190, 192, 195

R

Racism, racist 26, 153, 154
Ratio of negativity-positivity 200
Reis, Harry 157
Relaxation 13, 49, 51, 53, 54, 60, 61, 63-7, 69, 70, 72, 199, 207, 213
Repatriation 38, 39, 91
Resilience, resilient 12, 14, 22, 23, 25, 26, 30, 33, 48, 73, 84, 86, 87, 159, 194-7, 199-202, 207
Rizzolatti, Giacomo 143
Rose, Robert 28
Ryan, Richard 189

S

Sadness 25, 34, 52, 72, 81, 83, 85
Safety 24, 38, 75, 82
Sapolsky, Robert 59
School(s) 21, 24, 75, 78, 106, 107, 114, 122, 126-131, 133, 138, 141, 152, 163, 166, 168, 169, 182, 183, 207
Security 18, 82, 145, 175, 176, 199
Self-compassion 84, 199
Self-confidence 28, 32, 40, 49, 124, 157, 159, 172, 199
Self-criticism 84, 85
Self-determination

theory 189
Self-discovery 198
Self-esteem 36
Seligman, Martin 38, 86, 87, 200
Selye, Hans 55, 56
Separation 43, 151, 163, 165, 173, 175
Sex, sexual 45, 113, 114
Shame 44, 109, 161, 172
Short-term orientation 119, 120
Siegel, Daniel 49, 67, 85
Sign Language 126, 137
Silences 92, 140
Solitude 47, 48, 53, 189
Stereotype(s) 100, 124, 150, 151, 153, 154, 156, 157, 203
Strength(s) 3, 13, 23, 34, 41, 60, 82, 83, 88, 90, 161, 172, 188, 194, 198, 203, 207-9, 215, 216
Stress 10, 12, 14, 21-3, 26, 30, 32, 33, 38, 45, 51, 55-61, 63, 66, 70, 72-4, 76, 81, 90, 114, 146, 167, 168, 176, 191, 194, 198, 207
  Acculturation stress 3, 55
  Chronic stress 22, 23, 58-60, 81, 167, 191
  Short-term stress 59
  Stress management 12, 74, 207
  Stress reduction 60, 61, 146
  Stress response 56, 57
Stuck 11, 29, 33, 60, 81
Suicidal 146
Support

Emotional support 148, 168, 179
Invisible support 147, 148
Perceived support 147
Social support 48, 110, 145-9, 162, 195
Support networks 162
Sympathetic system 57

T

Teacher(s) 58, 101, 102, 122, 123, 126, 132, 141, 207
Therapy(ies) 14, 34, 70, 83, 146
Tolerance 114, 116, 154, 198
Transitivity 181
Trauma(s), traumatic 22, 48, 49, 58, 59, 85, 190, 194, 206, 207
Trust 11, 31, 85, 142, 157, 185
Tugade, Michele 30

U

Uncertainty(ies) 18, 116-8, 151, 155, 157
Unhappiness, unhappy 20, 33, 52, 53, 83, 84, 181
UN organizations 176

V

Values 17, 25, 33, 93, 95, 99, 100, 106, 107, 110, 112, 119, 122-5, 150, 154, 159, 163, 180, 184, 193, 199, 201

Victim(s) 11, 30, 31, 33, 52, 90, 194, 200
Visualisation 54, 60, 63, 65-7, 72, 199

W

War refugee 160
Well-being 4, 22, 25, 38, 40, 51, 84, 86, 87, 102, 124, 145, 149, 162, 164, 165, 175, 177, 188, 189, 194-7, 204
Westerners 97, 98, 140, 141
Wisdom 41, 119

Y

Yarbus, Alfred 94, 95, 99
Yoga 47, 51, 73

ACKNOWLEDGMENTS

My special thanks go to Andy Woods. Andy and his wife Johanna Kuenzel were my early supporters, and Andy has dedicated countless hours of his free time to build up the Expatscience.com website to enable me to spread the word and help me become a self-published author.

Many other people who helped me along the way also deserve a special mention:

Marissa van Uden carefully edited the final manuscript and helped me clarify my thoughts and sharpen my prose. Kathy Woods and Shana Aucsmith helped proofread and edit earlier versions of the manuscript. Siobhan Mitchell, Veronique Zancarini, Nel Mostert, and Linda A. Janssen helped me to improve my style and the manuscript flow.

Lorraine Boyle and Sylvia Weelen supported me in organizing parent workshops (Transition Workshops) in the international section of De Blijberg school in Rotterdam. Nel Mostert brought her professional skills to the workshops and facilitated the Transition Workshops in her free time.

Lucie Cunningham generously helped me build my network in the professional expat community.

I've been very touched by the interest and encouragement I received during the preparation of this book. I would like to thank all the people who took an interest in my work and offered their help by circulating my questionnaires by Internet.

Above all, my thanks go to the people (many of them anonymous) who took the time to share their international experience via the questionnaires and during the Transition Workshops.

ABOUT THE AUTHOR

Dr Catherine Transler, Ph.D, is a freelance writer and a researcher in psychology in a multinational company. She has a long history of living abroad and working in international teams. She started her career as a clinical psychologist in France. In 1999, she was awarded a European PhD in experimental psychology co-jointly from the Free University of Brussels (Belgium) and the University of Burgundy (France). She has lead projects involving the creation and adaptation of psychological tests and questionnaires to suit diverse populations ranging from deaf children in France, the UK and the Netherlands to school children and their families who live in slums in India. She now lives in the Netherlands.

Author online
For more resources,
visit Catherine's blog at
www.expatscience.com

www.ingramcontent.com/pod-product-compliance
Lightning Source LLC
Chambersburg PA
CBHW060506090426
42735CB00011B/2122